TAWANTINSUYO 5.0

Alonso del Río

Copyright © 2015 by Alonso del Río.

Cover design and weaving: Waltraut Stölben
General Editor: Fortunata Barrios
Design, graphics and layout: Claudia Sarmiento

First Edition: December 2007

ISBN: Softcover   978-1-4633-9775-3
               eBook   978-1-4633-9774-6

Print information available on the last page.

Rev. date: 22/10/2015

To order additional copies of this book, please contact:
Palibrio
1663 Liberty Drive
Suite 200
Bloomington, IN 47403
Toll Free from the U.S.A 877.407.5847
Toll Free from Mexico 01.800.288.2243
Toll Free from Spain 900.866.949
From other International locations +1.812.671.9757
Fax: 01.812.355.1576
orders@palibrio.com
471499

Contents

CHAPTER III   The Ternary   111

Acknowledgment

To my great mother and my great father —Pachamama and Pachakamaq—, for creating this marvel we call 'life'. To the Sun and the Moon, the sky and the earth, my grandparents. To my father and my mother, for the gift of existence and of love. To my great love Waldi, for a full life in the three worlds and for the opportunity to allow me to be honest. To my children, my teachers. To my unforgettable Don Benito, who protected me and guided me through the difficult path of sacred plants. To my lifelong friend, Fortunata Barrios, editor and midwife of this book. To Claudia Sarmiento, who drew the graphics and worked on the layout of this book with all of her love. To Zadir Milla, who provided some images and concepts on the Tawantinsuyo. To Román Vizcarra, who taught me the importance of speaking about the Tawantinsuyo with your own words. To my friends Rajani and Guillermo Pernas, who finally convinced me to write this book. And here would follow a long list of brothers and sisters from all around the world, with whom I have been very happy sharing many ceremonies, the fruits and reflections of which I present here. Last but not least, to all the men and women who walked before us the sacred American path and made it possible for that knowledge to arrive in our hands. I always have you all in my heart.

Chapter 0

This book gathers what I can share up to now after 30 years of walking the path of sacred plants and studying ancient symbols and traditions from remote times. My first teachers were from the Shipibo nation in the Peruvian Amazon. They instructed me in the art of the sacred medicine we call 'ayahuasca'. All my gratefulness to the Arévalo family and in particular to my unforgettable don Benito. My second source of learning was the traditions of the North American natives. Ceremonies like the Vision Quest, Sundance and the Inipi were a determining factor in my life to reconcile with myself and bring back the understanding of what it means to pray. My third thanks goes to the Tawantinsuyo Nation spread out in time and space but united like a monolith in its love for reality and common good. The teachers here were the stones, the temples, the textiles, the living culture and all the different designs that for millennia the ancient ones used to pass on so many truths that would not even fit in a 1000 page book.

If we represent total truth with a dot in the center of a circle, we would at least have 360 ways of looking at it. If we take into account the minutes and seconds that form each degree we could have 1,296,000 different approaches. This work does not even pretend to be one of those many points. Each being has the right to simply describe what they are seeing. This is simply my proposal in front of my family, in front of my brothers and sisters. I want to unfold if in front of you like a carpet. If it works for you, use it.

To my brothers that are Tawantinsuyo theorists, I ask for forgiveness for using controversial words for the Tawantinsuyan orthodoxy. Terms like 'God' or 'pray' have been included because I think they can help some people easily understand the text. I invoke inclusion, understanding. In any case, it is necessary to specify the meaning of 'God' as the 'cause without cause' and of 'praying' as 'to dialog in a sacred manner'.

I exonerate myself from any scientific pretension that this text might show. This is not a history or archeology book. There are scholars that have written about ancient Peru from the perspective of social sciences. Many of them agree that the wisdom of Andean and Amazonian peoples does not need to be validated in terms of modern science because even thousands of years before the word 'science' was coined, there was already in the Americas[1] surprising achievements in different areas of knowledge. This continent followed its own sacred path evolving in the search of the equilibrium between thinking and feeling. I find it arbitrary to ignore the singular values in which the American process is based in order to make it fit within the patterns of the development of the western model that, for example, labels the civilization that did not have writing as 'primitive'. One of the intentions of this book is precisely to revalue the symbol as a masterful means of communication. In some way, sometimes I even find it superior to writing because it is the merging of a rational concept with an emotional image. Highest wisdom. It is precisely an essential part of this work to take a look again at the relationship between feeling and reason, between feminine and masculine, not only to live as complete and balanced human beings but because this duality is the foundation of light, of life itself.

This book answers to the urgent necessity to switch the paradigm of 'spiritual evolution' for 'sacred path' since the former creates and absurd opposition between spirit and matter, not acknowledging the sacred quality of the latter. A society that is little conscious of the sacred dimension of the feminine is being developed, which generates disastrous consequences in the relationships between man and woman, and between human beings and mother earth. Some 'spiritualists' do not see matter or women or the planet as a sacred mother but as a thing.

---

1. Translators note: the word America relates to the whole American continent, what in the US it is commonly referred to as the Americas is called America in the rest of the continent.

On the other hand, herein lies the almost accomplished dream of talking about a great universal synthesis of human knowledge, expressed mostly in an integrating vision of the quadripartition, the wheel of medicine and the dynamic law of transformation. Three systems of transformation developed simultaneously in five different continents. Raising this fifth universal Tawantinsuyo we recognize the capability of all peoples and all beings to arrive at the same truths when we live 'with the heart in hand'.

The use of master plants was a fact of undeniable importance in ancient Peru and in my point of view plants have a much greater influence than geography when it comes to shaping the interior landscape of men and the culture that use them. It is not my intention to justify myself or give myself credit to try to validate my opinion. But I do want to say that essentially, my mind is more similar to that of a Chavin officiant than to many of my contemporaries.

I share with many researchers of the Andean culture the need to complement the female energy represented by Pachamama with its masculine counterpart. We know that Pachamama is also father and mother for the duality that every being has, but it is easy to realize that it is predominantly a feminine energy. *Pachamama* is the mother of the whole universe. Literally, the mother of Space. Therefore, following the great teaching of parity and complementarity in the Andean world, the big question is: where is the partner of Pachamama?

This absence is not part of the great mystery but of the huge empty gaps left by military and religious invaders after centuries of opprobrium and extermination. It is not my intention to fill in the gaps for the sake of filling them in order to have something complete to show. I do not feel that obligation. The subject inspires my utmost respect. The truth is that my search for equilibrium, harmony and complementarity asks me to give and image and a name to who I consider my father, my mother's partner, my lord Pachakamaq, father of Time. Literally 'creator of Time'. Only direct iconography and tradition collected in some cultures were able to free us from the immense error to mistake Pachakamaq with the supreme creator Wiraqocha. To those who continue to repeat this identification, complementarity could just be a 15-letter word because according to iconography, Wiraqocha represents the unity that contains the unmanifested duality. In this gigantic absence even of temples, rituals and memory, I find a tremendous and enormous presence that floods all that exists: Pachakamaq is also the spirit, my own spirit.

On the other hand, in moments in which diversity is seriously threatened, each culture has not only the right but the obligation to reconstruct their own natural form to relate to the sacred. All peoples and nations devastated by religious imperialisms must reconnect with the mere prayer that sprout from the core of every corner of our mother earth. I do not think there is a more powerful prayer in your land than that of your ancestors, even if you have to go back many centuries. I am not saying for us to invent or copy the past, nor that we attach to it. Each tradition and ritual is different because each part of the earth is different. The rites resonate with the culture and the geographical shape of each place and that is in part what gives these rites so much power.

I find it very interesting to know all traditions and ways of praying in the world but importing and exporting religions is not my thing. I invite people from the places where life takes me to find out the local way of praying and I do not intend to impose my way. Here in my land, I like to call my great mother and my great father by their traditional names but I think it is important that each culture recovers their own voice, making a last attempt to preserve one of the greatest gifts of this life: the great diversity of which you and I form a part.

In the first chapter I attempt to talk about unity and the great creator Wiraqocha who is beyond and above the three worlds. Then I continue with different reflections that can be useful to contextualize what comes next. In the second chapter the great subject is duality, Pachamama and Pachakamaq which in the *Kay pacha* are represented by man and woman. Within ourselves —*Uhu pacha*—Pachamama and Pachakamaq become mind and feeling, the last representatives of these primordial energies to which we dedicate a good amount of attention. In the third chapter I treat the three worlds, the triads, the trinities. Finally, in the fourth I aboard the Tawantinsuyo more like a concept than a historical reality. Then I talk about quadripartition and the wheel of medicine relating them to other similar systems in all continents. The analogies or images that I use are only means to translate totally abstract situations and realities into simpler understandings. They are not to be taken as beliefs that replace the reality they represent.

We are presently contemplating the manifestation of one of the most important myths of humanity: the Ouroboros, the serpent that bites its own tail. Many of the latest scientific discoveries only but prove the inexplicable wisdom of ancient times. How and through which ways did the ancient ones access such truths? This is one of the points I comment on towards the end of the fourth chapter when I talk about ayahuasca. In this book the word 'medicine' generally refers to all sacred plant or plants of power and in particular I use it for ayahuasca. This structure of four chapters was intuitively designed following the same fractal logic of the wheel of medicine or the dynamic law of transformation.

Lastly I will say that if my dream was completely fulfilled it would not be necessary to write this book. It would be enough to contemplate the design on the cover. Do not forget that what is written is only my interpretation; the truth is in the symbol, in the weaving…

Chapter I

Unity

The Chavin monument approximately 4000 years old represents Wiraqocha, creator of the world, flaunting two scepters. The two energies inside the hands symbolize the primordial energies —the masculine and the feminine— in potential state. All the adornments in the upper part could correspond to the innumerable worlds or dimensions it holds within.

The invisible path

I have no doubt that the ancient teaching speaks to us of two paths: one to go and one to return. A visible path and another one invisible, a path towards diversity and another towards unity, one towards the mind and another towards the heart, one towards knowledge and another towards wisdom.

This book is the beginning of the path of return. It is thought and felt for all those brothers and sisters that have intuited the end of the first path. Where else will you search? How much more information do you want to have? How big do you want to let your ego grow before you offer it up? If you believe you are mature enough and ready to begin the invisible path; that it is useless to continue filling yourself with information infinitely; that there is nowhere else to look but within; this is your book and it is made for you because it is written from within and we are all equal within. This is one of the secrets of unity.

If you are not ready to start on the path of return and you rightfully believe that you need more time to learn and enrich your personality, I implore you to not keep reading because further on you will maybe find phrases and truths that might offend your beliefs and that is by no means my intention. The teaching of the invisible path is many times contrary to the visible path and if you are not mature enough for the great journey of return, you will simply not understand or will not be able to handle the intensity of love and pain that these pages hide.

To talk about the great unity of all that exists is not just opening to the immeasurable love that is the sustenance of all existence but also opening to all the pain of all that suffers. It is about your sensitivity and the intensity with which you feel. If you think becoming immune to the suffering of others is an accomplishment, you are putting a limitation to your own capacity to love. Remember this well, your capacity to feel pain is the same as your capacity to feel love, it is exactly the same.

Love and pain are like the two wings given to us at the end of the path to go and without them it is impossible to fly on the path of return. Have you ever seen a bird flying with one wing?

The path of return has no rules, no time; if you see it, you have done it. There is no way to prepare yourself to walk it better because it is not to be walked, it is to be flown.

Absolute unity and relative unity

Everything that exists contains duality as part of its nature. Everything that exists will have its relative unity and its relative diversity, that is to say its feminine part and its masculine part and in this way each of these parts considered as a unity will have their own duality.

To have a sense of the absolute unity, the unity of all that exists, including what could exist is only possible through feeling. The mind is of no use for this. It is not enough to imagine unity. Most cultures that reflected on it coincided in that it is beyond the human mind. Nonetheless, each culture gave it a name in their own language with words that meant more or less the same: the inaccessible, the incomprehensible, the great mystery, the cause without cause. What is true is that the concept of unity of all that exists can be perceived by the mind in different levels of clarity but can only be perceived in its totality only by the heart. To be able to fully perceive unity, we cannot keep thinking in the same way; moreover, we cannot keep thinking, we have to feel it. The more we think 'I want to understand unity' the more incomprehensible it will be. Because our mind is saying 'me and unity'. In order to fully feel unity, there cannot be a mind that names, a belief that creates distance nor a religion that separates. We have to be willing to renounce all religion, all belief and all thought.

Our search starts with a simple question: 'Who am I?' If we are lucky to not answer immediately from our conditioning and we let this question rest within ourselves, the answer will fall one day like a mature fruit that will nurture us and make us happy for life. At times my desire to express the answer is almost uncontrollable, but I find more satisfaction in spreading out all the pieces so that each person makes their own search. On the other hand, to describe it in simple words would not help much.

Which is the biggest obstacle to understand such a simple yet complex teaching? To begin with, I believe it is very difficult to understand something 'outside' if its analogy has not been understood 'inside'. The ideas I can transmit to you and in general, any teaching; you cannot know them but you can recognize them; firstly they have to exist inside yourself. You have to have lived certain experiences so that what you read resonates in you. If the experience does not exist within you, you will not have the image in your mind and what I say will be empty; you will only imagine that you understand it. If you understand what I say is because you already know it. You know it but it is in a more profound level of your life and not in the surface of the intellect.

I only remind you, I make it resonate within you. Resonate. This word is very important, it is a whole science, we have to learn to resonate. For example, when we tune a musical instrument we do it by resonance. That is to say we level the vibration of the model source with the instrument we want to tune. When we talk of the A440 note, we are referring to the sound emitted by a sound source when it vibrates 440 times per second — this is the frequency with which it vibrates—. This note will have multiples going up and down. That is to say, there will be an A440, another 110 and a 55. In the same way, an A880 and so on going up. Truths, concepts and understandings work in a similar way. Original truths emit a vibration that we make resonate —in the multiple that corresponds to each one of us— matching our vibration to the exact frequency. That is clarity. We must adapt to the truth, not adapt truth to our interests.

When a person establishes herself in knowledge, she recognizes the happiness in not harming any form of life. In this way, she completes the first stage. But she cannot be an island in a sea of suffering so she will soon realize that his happiness has a limit; she cannot grow more because she is being squeezed by the pain of 'others' and feels she needs to start to alleviate and share that pain that surrounds her. She is not doing this because she wants to be 'good' or 'altruist' but because the final truth is *we are all one*. Such phrase looks easy written in italics and yet how difficult it is to demonstrate. Isn't it paradoxical? The oldest, greatest and most difficult teaching of the peoples of the Americas was: *I am you, you are me*. There were only three words to express the biggest mystery of existence; the unity of all that exists.

How to meditate in unity, how do we try to feel it if we are still angry with someone else? It is necessary to have worked very seriously on forgiveness, to have forgiven everybody from the depth of our being. So in this way when the time comes to invoke unity, no thoughts of excluding somebody will rise. If we are capable to observe that there are great discrepancies and contradictions within us, how can we not understand and forgive when they exist in others?

Offenses are something that stop us from feeling unity. When somebody hurts us, it activates one of the most powerful and difficult to control patterns, even more so when it is a totally unjust offense. There is nothing more hurtful than injustice. To reject injustice is one of the proper and noble thoughts of the human race. However, even this thought becomes and obstacle when we try to dive into the mystery of unity. How difficult it is to reconcile with somebody that has offended us unjustly, more so when they do not show signs of repentance or of recognizing the error. This marvelous mystery that is life asks us to be tolerant even with the intolerant ones and to be honest even with the liars. We can continue to have discrepancies about many things with many people, but we cannot continue offending or allowing to be offended. How many thoughts we have to discard, how much pride we have to throw away before we let go of that emotion of being an offended victim and simply understand and forgive. Forgive not because it is good or this or that religion orders so. Forgive because it is the end of the path, the only exit, the end of the mind. Forgive because it is the path to freedom, to unity.

Illa Teqse Wiraqocha

The great creator, the cause without cause, previous to all manifestation they called Wiraqocha and they intuitively related him/her to light. Only recently quantum physics reveals the mystery of the dual nature of light —waving or corpuscles particles— and the answer is that it has both. The understanding of the human being reaches a height to be able to imagine a creator that has a dual nature: masculine-feminine, absolute-relative, manifested-unmanifested, etc., etc. However, this was known in America 5000 years ago. This hint science gives us is a determining factor to be able to understand the whole history of creation and not get trapped in the dogmatism of any one school.

When faced with an almost total emptiness of information, many people get tremendously confused about which properties and attributes they can give to the three great characters of Andean cosmology: Wiraqocha, Pachamama and Pachakamaq. Some even turn Pachamama into masculine energy to make it fit with the description of the altar to Qorikancha, others confuse Wiraqocha with Pachakamaq. Anyhow, there is an endless number of versions and almost eternal explanations.

Another version of creator, expressed by Tiawanko culture in the so called Gate of the Sun in Bolivia. Always holding the two scepters, lord of duality.

This symbol is more than clear to me. Wiraqocha represents duality in its power —that is why it holds a scepter in each hand—. He/she is still not letting go of it, he/she does not manifest it, but he/she does contain it. It is an existence prior to the separation of energies, it exists in the unfathomable universe of the preterit unity symbolized by light, and because of that it is Wiraqocha. *Wira* refers to the fire —the popular meaning is the grease that burns in a lamp— and *qocha* —literally 'lagoon'— makes reference to water. It is a beautiful and poetic image of a sacred and inextinguishable fire burning on the water. The complete name of the creator in the Andean worlds is: *Illa Teqse Wiraqocha*. Illa means 'light', *Teqse* means 'foundation'. Free translation: 'The sacred foundation of light'. *Wiraqocha* is the union of the masculine and the feminine. The negative and positive poles are the foundation of light. Pure science.

The paradox

I do not believe there is a term in any language that can describe life but if I had to choose one I would choose the word 'paradox'. Life is a paradox from every angle we look at it. It is paradoxical that we have to start speaking about unity when it just happens to be the final conclusion of the understanding and the goal of all our efforts. How can I explain what can only be comprehended when you finish understanding? How can I start to explain how sacred the things I want to say are when the dimension of the sacred is maybe just a seed within you? Is it not paradoxical that when you are starting to enjoy and understand the mystery of life in this planet you already have to depart? That the biggest teacher in life is error? That you cannot rewind the movie and do things right from the beginning? Why does it hurt so much to recognize true love? I have a long list of questions and I imagine each person has their own but the answer that fits perfectly for all of them is: holy paradox.

The mind has as its intrinsic nature the duality masked as exquisite paradox. The consequences of bad mind management are conflict and confrontation. To win the match against the mind, we have to enter its game. That is to say, divide the duality that mind proposes. We call this the *dual division*, the essence of quadripartition. To create our own paradox within the paradox.

The numbers

The numbers are only values or figures that work to count or measure. They are mainly archetypes, particularly the first ones. They express very profound philosophical concepts that have always been a subject of study in different cultures. They express models of relationships among themselves, closed systems, complete universes.

A dual system will never be equal to a Trinitarian one nor to one where quadripartition governs. No system is superior to another. Each one —even those of six or seven dimensions— has its own reason to be and its specific applications. To try to confront the systems like one was superior to another is part of the redundant vice of dual logic. To think that the Chinese system of five elements is superior to the American of four —which coincided with Plato's— and to believe that both of them are inferior to trinity is a sample of little understanding. It is naïve to believe that we are going to resolve the mystery of divinity and its sacred origin by discussing which of the systems is superior. Not everything is always in opposition and exclusion.

We can consider each number as a complete universe and the whole numeric system as a system of dimensions. But I also see them as a system that connects each number with different types of relationship. Inside the compartment of unique things I keep everything that is unique, that with which I keep a unique relationship: my father's love, my mother's love, my couple relationship. I keep all that I perceive as dual in this life in the compartment of duality, everything that has a pair, which has two sides: my understandings, emotions, concepts, beliefs, judgments, etc. In the compartment that has room for three, all that is Trinitarian, all types of relationships or systems that have three elements: family (father, mother, son); the three Andean worlds (*Hanan*, *Kay* y *Uhu pacha*); the past, present and future. Inside the one that has four, the four directions, the four elements; practically everything because the whole can be understood through number four according to the marvelous teaching of master Pythagoras and his famous *tetraktys*. And in this way each number holds a particular quality.

Fractal understanding

I have taken from the Wikipedia encyclopedia online the following definition of a fractal:

> A fractal is a geometric object whose basic structure repeats in different scales. The term was coined by mathematician Benoit Madelbrot in 1975. In many cases fractals can be generated by a process of recursion or iteration capable of producing self-similarity structures independently of the specific scale. Fractals are geometric structures that combine irregularity and structure. Many natural structures have fractal type structures, they have details in scales arbitrarily small.

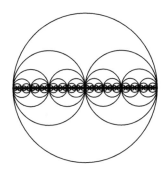

For our practical application of this theory, one of the main things worth underlying is the perfect and harmonious relationship of the whole with the part. The part is the perfect expression of the whole and vice versa.

In ancient times many cultures understood and used what nowadays is known as 'fractal theory'. It is a natural law, it is the way in which the universe is created and developed. To understand what is a fractal is absolutely essential in order to understand this book because its structure is precisely a fractal.

The best way is to consider a fractal process. We will start with a very simple one. If we divide an imaginary line, thus determining two equal parts, these represent for us the two original energies, opposite and complementary. Of the two segments, if one represents unity the other will express diversity and will immediately divide itself in two parts. Of the segment that was divided, one will continue to represent unity and the other will again divide itself representing diversity and so on and so forth infinitely. From this we deduce that the concepts of masculine and feminine associated with unity and diversity are totally and absolutely relative. Only the first archetypical couple —the first line— is understood as absolute masculine and absolute feminine. After the first line we are all relative masculine and feminine.

Principle of diversity   Principle of unity

Another fractal principle is the quaternary, which arises from the dual division or the division of duality. The four dimensions within which our existence happens are this quaternary. Once the vertical axis and the horizontal axis cross each other forming a Cartesian plane, they generate four spaces and each one of them will produce another quaternary. All this understanding was expressed in ancient times in textiles, ceramic and architecture.

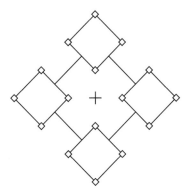

Another classic fractal of ancient times is the well-known Tarot game. It seems that the ancient sages of the middle east decided to make an experiment: 'to encrypt' inside a divinatory game concepts of the highest value that can survive the passing of centuries and in this way, prevent this wisdom from remote times from getting lost. The philosophical part —not the recreational— represents a cosmic law that reduces all the numbers to the first three, awarding them three types of values —positive, negative and neutral— considering the fourth also as positive, but considered negative as part of the second triad with relation to the first, in a way that the first ternary is positive and the second one is negative.

	Positive	Negative	Neutral	
First Ternary	1	2	3	Positive
Second Ternary	4	5	6	Negative
Third Ternary	7	8	9	Neutral

Then, if we consider this first septenary as a unity it will be positive and the second septenary will be negative in relation to the first. This is a good model of fractal construction. I do not intend to dedicate any more time to this now but I will say that this simple game deserves to be taken a little more seriously.

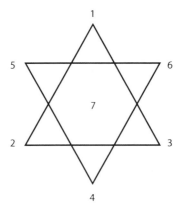

Masters and paths

'You can deceive a man all the time,
you can deceive everybody for some time,
but you can't deceive everybody all the time'.

Benjamin Franklin

They say that light is created first and then the eyes that observe it. In the same way, in human groups and societies, teachers arise to satisfy a natural and specific need in each case. Thus, there are so many masters of such variety of caliber and understanding. A master can be simply that person that helps you take the next step. But it is each person's job and responsibility to know when to continue and when to abandon certain circles once the lesson has been learned. In present times, to be a 'master' or a 'guru' has become a very profitable business (the United States is one of the countries with the largest number of sects, religions, masters and gurus). It is of utmost importance to have our eyes wide open looking within and without. Sometimes it is very difficult to distinguish the true ones from the false ones because the latter ones have good disguises and even achieve small powers that can deceive and 'in some way' complicate our paths a little. Their lies are very well staged and they almost seem real. Therefore it is more important to look within very attentively, towards our own lie because this is what in the end will bring us to connect by *resonance* with similar people with similar lies.

One of the aspects of these 'masters' that is quite hard to understand is that for the most part they are good people who can have good achievements and good work but their main mistake is they try to hide their flaws and sell an image that is not accurate. The need to find help in an instructor makes people idealize teachers and believe they are accomplished and perfect. And in this case, silence is an affirmation. Anyone that agrees to a wrong opinion of themselves is contributing to the mistake. It is important that each instructor or elder brother changes their strategy sharing their flaws or their limitations, placing them in the open instead of spending so much energy trying to hide them, thinking that to admit mistakes will weaken the faith of their believers. Quite on the contrary, only the liars and the ones that love appearances will move away; the others will be captivated by honesty.

Society has been polarized in disciples and masters. There are no intermediate levels. As soon as they learn four things they call themselves masters, gurus or medicine men. My way of learning is mostly observing nature, reality. Everything is gradual in it. The sun does not generally burst in at midnight like if it was noon and gives us 'illumination' unless we have spent all day in a dark room.

In order to find truth first you have to find your lie. If we cannot see the lie within us, it will be very difficult to see it without. Everything is connected through very subtle threads and we often unconsciously play the game of feeding the lie of somebody that feeds ours. In all our relationships we have to learn to recognize that mental pattern which is very negative for our development. To not feed anybody's lie nor let anybody feed ours.

In this way we see that one of the most widely used techniques to gain adepts is to make them feel 'special', 'the sect of the chosen ones'. But if one is doing a little more serious work, one will reject any kind of adulation of the ego and will never be hooked by these people or will realize pretty soon what the true intentions are. We can also look at it in a different way. There are teachers of many kinds. Some can teach showing *what to do* while others teach *what not to do*. Sometimes it seems that the latter ones are more efficient. In fact, they are larger in numbers and from them I have received teachings I am very grateful for but I personally prefer the other kind.

A tale says that many years ago in the city of Varanasi, India, lived a man of middle age that was seeking the perfect business to get rich as fast as possible. Every honest enterprise that he started seemed to him insufficiently profitable until one day, wandering through downtown he saw a skinny blind beggar sitting in lotus position begging for money. The man gave him a coin and he lifted a small dirty sign that read 'thank you', indicating thus that being mute was another of his misfortunes. The man suddenly came up with and idea for the business he had been waiting for. He took the beggar home, cleaned him, bought impeccable white clothes for him, combed his hair and his long beard. Once finished he seated him in the center of the living room on a beautiful and soft red velvet cushion. The beggar had been transformed into a true guru, at least in appearance. He quickly called all his friends and family members telling them he had been blessed with the presence of a great master that had incredible healing powers and only communicated through him via telepathy. People started coming to meet this great guru and many said they left very alleviated after meditating in his presence for several hours. Even one person that had been in a wheelchair for more than ten years stood up and walked and everybody yelled: 'it's a miracle, it's a miracle'. His fame was growing day by day and so were the donations and offerings. The businessman finally fulfilled his dream and became a big millionaire. One day, the great Maharaja of Varanasi showed up at his door, an immensely rich man who besides being sincere and merciful, was known throughout the whole country for his generous and detached soul and was following the spiritual path. He came before the 'disciple' of the great guru and told him that after having shared time with the great masters of all around India, he felt his life was stuck and he needed to revitalize his faith. They went together in front of the guru and after several minutes sitting in silence the 'disciple' said: 'the teacher says that you lead a beautiful spiritual life and you are very close to attaining enlightment but you only need to pass the most difficult test: total renouncement'. The maharaja left and meditated all night on the words of the great teacher. The next day he came back to see the guru and told him: 'I have deeply reflected and reached the conclusion that you are a wise man and I know clearly which my next step is'. And making a pause, he added: 'I left a small fortune that will support my family and I will donate my immense richness with all the palaces included for you to administer it and I will sit at your feet and start my life as a renunciate'. The businessman could hardly keep calm with such statement but he contained himself until the maharaja left announcing that he was going to transfer all his wealth immediately. The maharaja kept his word, he got rid of everything he owned and spent the night praying in the woods. In the middle of the night, the very lord Vishnu appeared to him and told him: 'here is a man with a pure heart. I will gift you great and glorious days on this earth and starting today people will call you 'the enlightened one from the woods'. I also have to tell you that that 'master' you venerate is not a real guru. He is just a beggar and his 'disciple' is a swindler that takes advantage of the good faith of people, but without them knowing about it I use them and they serve me".

The fact that the world and the 'spiritual path' are full of liars does not change what is essential. We have to learn to trust. A thousand times I have been deceived and a thousand and one times I will trust again. I do not know any other way, my path is to trust and open myself, dissolve all barriers, all protections.

In the last few decades of this splendorous civilization, the ostentation of 'our spiritual path' has become one of the most precious jewels of the ego. 'I'm a Buddhist', 'I'm Sufi', 'I'm also a Buddhist but form another branch', 'I'm of the fourth path', 'I'm of the fifth path', 'I'm from the red path', in this way the market has found a new mine in 'spirituality'. Hundreds and hundreds of paths and gurus, workshops for growth and evolution —from the most *light* to the most ridiculous— compete in the market of incautious souls. Also thousands of books, many of them *best sellers* full of nothing, only the death of thousand of trees made into paper. Even the film industry is making profitable spiritual movies now. Spirituality is on vogue.

On the other hand, the demand grows of millions of people seeking something that is only inside themselves but they naively seek outside or in someone that will sell them a secret, a formula, an exercise, a mantra, a 'spiritual name', a song or a book that makes them happy or changes their lives. They are willing to spend according to their means, enormous amounts of money. As long as you do not stop your self-deceit, you will be prey of all kinds of deceivers.

I met a man that boasted he spent several hundred thousand dollars in courses and workshops. He even talked about a very exclusive one with I don't know who that cost like 30000 dollars. Two weeks in a luxurious cruise. When he told me this, I could not avoid wondering how he might have been before his expensive 'spiritual transformation'.

It has taken me many years to arrive happily and smiling to the point to get rid of so much useless belief, of so much lie disguised as belief, philosophy, method or spiritual path. A true evolutionary method cannot be frozen, canned or be sold in a supermarket. Moreover, to talk about an 'evolutionary method' is in itself a major absurdity. Both words are contradictory by nature. Evolution is life and life will never be attained or understood through any method. The method is for the mind. There is a method to learn piano and one to learn Chinese but there is none and there cannot be one to learn life. The one that claims to have it is a swindler. Of course it is good to develop the mind and learn piano and Chinese. Developing the mind is part of the evolutionary plan, but do not confuse it with your own evolution, with your transformation, with the awakening of your consciousness. The problem arises again, when with that small part of our being called mind we try to encircle, understand and systematize the mystery of existence, the mystery of life.

I do not believe there is anything immovable or definite within the absolute relativity of this existence. Nor even my own tale. I always question it, reconsider it, reinvent it but it continues to be the same. In the end, it is just another proposal.

Change of axis

While reading a book that relates ancient stories of the migrations of the Hopi people, I soon recognized a profound symbolism hidden in the legend. I immediately thought of relating it with the following diagram. If we place ourselves in the center of this wheel of medicine and we decide to explore the four corners of the universe, the graphic of our route could be the one inside the circle.

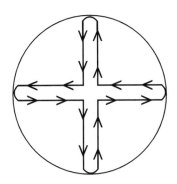

The Hopis tell that the four clans were sent to the four directions of the universe with the intention to obtain knowledge so they would reunite again and share what was learned. Our mission is to get as far as possible in the path of each direction, find wisdom, medicine, mystery and the power of each of them. Then find the return path to the center and depart again, start again the exploration of another direction, another dimension.

Some of the most important events that happen to us in the development of these 'migrations' are the changes of axis. I relate the horizontal axis with existence and the vertical one with love. If we follow this route, when we complete our fourth migration we will have changed axis four times. A change of axis represents a radical reconsideration of our priorities.

Lets imagine we part on our first migration towards the west, the direction of the mind: its element is water and its sacred word 'know'. It is the ocean of knowledge, of personality. We initiate this path with the best of intentions: to obtain a lot of knowledge to help all brothers and sisters. But sometimes it is difficult to determine how much knowledge we must accumulate and how much we must develop to start to share it or to serve others. When one says 'enough of growing, now it is time to give', one can be starting the path of return from the first migration. In this second stage we must dedicate more attention to feeling than thinking. The mind looses space and it is good to start knowing the other side of the pendulum. When all of a sudden we know it is not important to win more arguments or impose our ideas if this implies loosing contact with that beautiful feeling that emerges from the depth of our being, then we can say we have accomplished the first change of axis. Once this dimension of feeling is explored, when our being has been able to go beyond mind and reason many times, we have learned to enjoy *feeling*.

We then return to the axis of existence —second change of axis— we go from feeling to doing. We start our third migration. We recover the importance of the mental function, we can think about good actions and projects that help balance the world and share with those that were not as fortunate as us. We stop believing that what we feel is all that matters and we take a step into a new dimension of action, our third migration. Always including everything we learned previously, we achieve doing without doing, we do but we do not get entangled.

Then, with thought and action purified, in total harmony with what we feel, our fourth migration starts until we understand the mystery of quadripartition after walking for a long time in this direction. We can say that we have completed our fourth migration and closed the circle. What we feel, think, say and do is one thing. It does not matter anymore if we are dedicated to great projects or if we live in a cave in the Himalayas or in the depth of the Amazon jungle. Our existence and our love have been taken to the limit.

We have completed the great turn of the wheel of medicine. However, it is good to know that the turn of this great wheel is not all that exists —that it will probably take a lifetime— but that in a fractal way there are thousands or millions of small wheels that are small opportunities to align these four manifestations: what I feel, what I think, what I say and what I do.

Trust

Stop reading for a few seconds and feel what is moving inside of you. I do not know exactly what to call it. Energy? Spirit? Life? It does not matter. It moves and it makes us feel many things. Sometimes it moves so much that it expresses through tears of emotion or of gratitude to life. In some occasions the movement is fast, in others it is slow but when it stops for a long time we get sick. What stops this movement? What paralyzes us? There can be many apparent causes but frequently the root is fear. Many things can cause us fear. There can be fears of different intensities. A small fear is a small sickness; a big fear, a big one. Fear or sickness will always be an invitation to grow in the opposite, which is trust. Trust opposes fear like light to darkness. Where there is trust, there cannot be fear, same as where there is light there cannot be darkness. It is necessary to learn to trust.

The final truth —to the extent I can understand— the purpose of life is simply love. We have to trust the purpose of existence is love. Everything that exists, it exists because of love and for love. To achieve this unconditional love established in us on every level and that this truth accompanies us every instant will be our attempt for all our life. When I leave my house in a clear night and I see millions of stars, my eyes get misty in front of the mystery. To contemplate so much greatness, so much immensity. What did they do all of this for? Is all this waste of energy made with so much beauty and creativity simply a product of chance, of chaos? Or is there an intelligence capable of not only creating millions of stars, but also an intricate and complex web of relationships among all that exists? Everything, absolutely everything from a small virus to a great galaxy is part of a whole that we call creation. And this creation hides behind itself and beyond all its cruel appearance the secret best kept at the end of this labyrinth: the purpose of life is love and love is life. We have to learn to trust it is like that.

Part of the big mistake lies in that they have made us believe that we 'fell' from a more elevated 'spiritual' position, that we were thrown out of a privileged place and now we are in a place of punishment deprived of divine presence, almost like in a prison-planet. When they invented all these biblical fables about the origin of man, they did not do it with bad intentions but the result was disastrous. This lost paradise myth —highly negative in my point of view— has created in human beings a kind of longing for a perfect life full of marvelous situations that we can never achieve. This generates a permanent frustration that leads us to do transgressions and in some cases to show the worst of us to try to make good situations everlasting and live only in pleasure —one of the sides of duality— without accepting life just as it is: love and pain. Life has hard and difficult moments that are exactly there to bring out the best in each person, so that one day we can really express the purpose of life: love.

We have been creating almost by accident, a society that is the empire of fear to the point that even the unknown scares us. Fear is the best way to control each other. Lets look at it closely. From a healthy perspective, the unknown should not scare us but it terrifies us. Strangers scare us, different ones, different religions and cultures not to mention death. I do not believe that somebody who talks about death can be listened to for a long time, particularly if he does not promise eternal life and reincarnations. The dominant culture of today has not only taught us to be scared and never love the mystery, the unknown; even less to trust. The world, our parents, our schools teach to distrust to protect ourselves, to prevent, it does not matter from what or for what, simply because it is 'safer'.

Few people have an idea of a nation's expenses generated by the laws to avoid corruption, now that it is spread out and it affects both 'developing' countries as much as 'developed ones'. Corruption produces so much distrust that makes innumerable controls necessary and they end up choking economies. Corruption generates distrust, it paralyzes and sickens society whereas trust makes all energies flow, including economy.

From the first time somebody lied to us or betrayed us, it created the mental pattern that taught us to distrust in order to protect ourselves. But this is not the way out. The more fences of protection we raise between us and life, the more we move away from it, the more we get paralyzed and sick. I discovered many years ago that my calling is to trust and there is no other way. The solution is not in closing up but in opening. Of course it hurts but there is no other way.

When our energy finally gets paralyzed and we get sick, an emergency system activates and makes us sensitive through pain and thus we understand many things we were not able to comprehend before, particularly the healing message that sprouts from within us: the 'why' of our disease. What we need when we get sick is to detect with as much clarity as possible which is the fear that is paralyzing us and what we are afraid of. On the other hand, it is not only fear that paralyzes and sickens us. Many times it is a profound, sincere and visceral rejection of particular situations we have to face which are extremely difficult for us to handle. The blockage of our energy is produced by a sharp contradiction: a part of us wants one thing and the other part wants something else. Many times it is not just about choosing one and discarding the other. Sometimes it is a matter of holding up the necessary amount of time until life itself puts things in order, obviously with our help. The seriousness of the disease can depend on how long and how intense this conflict is.

All healing coming from the outside will only be a palliative and the disease will return eventually, probably with different symptoms. The true healing has to come necessarily from within. Of course we can and we will receive all kinds of help but if we do not make the effort to inquire with maximum sincerity into the depth of why we feel sick, the discomfort will keep trying to manifest and communicate its message of displeasure and dissatisfaction through different symptoms, until we pay attention to it. When the sickness manifests we must perceive what it is that paralyzes us. What is it we are not accepting? What are we rejecting? At this moment we must resort to all agents capable of moving our energy and return movement. Lets stop for a moment to consider this. What is it that moves us? What agents cause movement within us?

Everything certainly affects us in different ways and with different intensity. We can listen to a song or something funny, read a poem or a book that makes us think, go on a trip, receive love from our friends or our loved ones. All these have the ability to return movement to us and help us recover health. Other remedies and therapies work in the same way. They all aim to mobilize our energies, from acupuncture to floral remedies and even chemicals. The difference is that different therapies demand different levels of patient participation. Natural ones are more advisable because they motivate and require the presence of the internal doctor while chemicals turn the sick one more passive and abusing them ends up debilitating the immune system.

The myth of communication

Words can be like little empty boxes that our parents give to us when we are children and life colors them and fills them with content. Many times, in the understanding of our relationships with other people we assume that words mean the same for everybody. This is one of the many big lies or inaccuracies on which we build our lives: we assume the meaning we give to a word is the same for us and for everybody else. The importance of language does not have to be a matter of just linguists and philologists, but of every person that takes seriously the responsibility of trying to communicate with another human being.

When I talk to somebody I concentrate all my attention and intensity I am capable of as if I was in a sacred place in front of a powerful altar. I try *not* to chat superficially. Therefore it happens that within a few minutes of starting a conversation with people I just met, I suddenly find myself in the very center of their lives listening to their best-kept secrets. Many times their eyes get misty or full of tears because of this deep contact from being to being and I feel them say: 'finally someone saw me, someone touched me, someone listened to me, someone who doesn't want to convince me, manipulate me, control me; someone who doesn't want to sell me anything'. A very sacred moment is created then. For many years I have looked for the key word that allows relationships to recover their real and sacred nature. Two human beings must seat together to *share*, not to try to subdue each other. Many times, when it is perceived that someone does not have the intention to impose their own vision, they are either considered weak or that they are lacking in clarity. On the contrary, for me it is about a deep coherent respect with this approach: I have come to share and propose.

Going back to the words, I was saying that we are wrong assuming they have the same meaning for everybody. Lets look at some examples. When we want to express gratefulness we say 'thanks'. Yes, but what does this mean? For some it will be an empty word without emotion, a social formality; for others it will be what fills their heart with blessings. Lets take the word 'love'. Of what love are we talking about? Each one will understand it according to their own capacity to love and with relation to their own conditioned love. Lets take the word 'son'. For some it will be the most sacred reason of existence, the greatest force to be happy and to transform; for others it can be one more limitation to their 'freedom', an obstacle in their career or something that can be abandoned. This always has to be remembered in order to improve our communication and take precautions to be able to truly transmit what we want.

Another important thing that only happens in interpersonal communication is the need for a positive emotional relationship with the listener. Otherwise every word can be interpreted in the worse way. I have seen this in many couples with a bad relationship. Any word can be interpreted in the worse manner. If the person made enemies or is not well disposed with us it is best to wait for another time. The ideal scenario to communicate something is to create a relaxed environment, even with true tenderness. Otherwise the mental patterns of the listener will distort a great part of what we say. Besides, half or more than half of what we want to say will not be transmitted through words but through our vibration, for this reason it is essential to invoke a humble attitude form the beginning.

Now lets take a look at the whole process of communication. Not everything I wish to communicate is in words exactly like they sound in my mind. There are perceptions, sensations, intuitions that I wish to communicate but first I need to codify them, translate them into words. But lets remember that words have a special meaning for each person so even if I try to contextualize them to get greater definition and greater clarity, they will always be *my words* and I will always need more words to explain them. Then *my words* are loaded again with meaning by the listener according to their experience and in turn translate them to sensations, perceptions, intuitions, etc. apart from the filter represented by the subjective charge that allows agreeing or not with those words. So finally it is truly little what we can capture of the attempt that another being makes to communicate. Better take it as poetry. A friend of mine used to say: 'The only thing we agree on is that we don't agree on anything but this is already a good agreement'. At least he was sincere.

A large part of the attempts to communicate happen from an unconscious desire to manipulate the listener, considering him/her silly enough to not be able to discover the hidden interests or the incoherence, or the self-deceit of the one trying to communicate. We have to decide! Do we want to communicate or we want to play three-cushion billiards? I am not saying there are always bad intentions but as long as the person trying to communicate is still living in a deep self-deceit, there will not be any communication but a mockery. One of the things that have surprised me the most throughout my life is all the damage generated by misunderstandings. Everyone hears what they want to hear, or don't hear what they don't want to. Hence, when one really wants to understand, one understands even when things are explained upside down.

These apparent difficulties in communication do not take away the meaning nor they invalidate the attempt. It has to be a sacred act and it has to be practiced. On the other hand there are people that —thanks heaven— do manage similar meanings for the same words with which in different measures we can try to communicate.

Ricardo Espinosa, 'The Walker' sums up in a brushstroke this entire wording about words. At the end of an ayahuasca ceremony that had started with an inspired and flowered prayer in which I was trying to transmit to him many things I thought and felt, he said to me with a smile: 'even though everything you said is irrelevant, I still agree'. He grasped in a great and amazing way the true message behind every well-intentioned word: love, unity.

We are all like pebbles that keep rolling through the river of existence, crashing and transforming each other like an inevitable event, without any ill intention. Lets be very grateful for all the strikes to our friends, and specially to our not so friends, to all those voices that at some point tried to propose something to us that did not ignore our ignorance. We need to arrive at a deep, real place that works to come to agreements and, truly together, build a better society. We need to redefine many words so that the most important ones get back if not the same at least a similar meaning for a large number of people.

CHAPTER II

The great duality

Image of the known 4000 years old Chavin spear, it expresses manifested duality: with one hand it points to 'father' sky and with the other to 'mother' earth.

Pachamama and Pachakamaq

I understand the word 'God' as the cause without cause, the creator of the great duality. *There is no more reality than God and above all, there is no more God than reality.* I am happy to live in these times and to not be scared to publish this sentence. 'Primitive' cultures of the Americas lived it in all its dimension and depth. My 'grandparents' from the Tawantinsuyo were not that lucky. Many of them were tortured because they kept affirming that the Sun is our father and the Earth our mother. They created religions for the peoples based on the understanding of a fractal retro projection of reality. That is to say, after carefully observing reality they dared to deduce how and which are the roots of the great tree of existence. They based their religion and their metaphysical vision in the observation of reality, understanding —through the fractal concept— how the primordial energies descend plane by plane, level by level from the archetypes —like the great Father and the great Mother— to the last projections in the ends of creation: Sun and Moon, heaven and earth, our father and our mother until it reaches us creating our mind and our feeling, the masculine and the feminine.

Ancient Andean sages created a natural religion by analogy: 'as above so bellow'. Upon seeing that practically everything in nature has a father and a mother, they understood that the universe could not escape this concept. They named the great father Pachakamaq, the maker of Time and the great mother Pachamama, mother of Space. These two concepts give us a clue as to the depth of their meditations and their understanding, referring not to fable characters but to ultimate realities that form existence: Space and Time.

The term *pacha* in *runasimi* —Quechua people language— could mean both things; sometimes it was 'space', sometimes 'time' and sometimes 'space-time'. I stand in the line of all the human beings that recognize ourselves as offspring from the love between Space and Time, the divine couple. From this I understand Pachamama as 'the mother of the whole universe', actually as the whole universe and not just as mother earth, a diminished version of reality. Of course it is also our mother earth. In present days, even tradition teaches to recognize and honor the 'pachamamita' of the place one lives in, that little piece of earth that sustains us and provides food. But it is this and much more: not only all the feminine in the planet is Pachamama, all women and mothers, but every individual as creation is also part of Pachamama.

Parity

One of the biggest contributions of Tawantinsuyo culture to the universal culture is the dual view of the universe, of all that exists which is captured in abundant iconography since its beginning, in stone sculptures, ceramics and abundant textiles. What for many people were simple ornamental designs was for those that knew the tradition a constant permanent reminder that everything is dual in this world we call *Kay pacha*, everything has two sides.

Reality is formed by two opposing and complementary visions reminding us that things are not only how we see them, but we have to necessarily include the opposing and complementary vision. The strength of these symbols has the capability to pierce any mind regardless of how hard it is and open its path to the heart.

From a remote time, a perpetual questioning: which is the background and which is the form? Who is upside down?

For several years I contemplated almost without meaning to, this symbol that is painted in a wall of my house in front of the place where I usually sit. After a few months these 'little ducks' —that is how I call them warmly— started to talk to me and now they are 'my masters'. Which is the background and which is the form? Am I seeing things fine or am I seeing them upside down? These are questions that we should never abandon. As much as you think you are seeing things fine there will always be and opposing and complementary view as part of reality.

The symbolic reality

Incan *Tokapu* that represents the stairs
—space— and the spiral —time—.

Every time I observe this symbol (stairs and spiral) that to my understanding is the simplest and one of the most sacred ones, I never stop being amazed by and grateful to the men that lived in the Americas thousands of years ago and chose this marvelous option to transmit their profound understanding of life. Communication through symbols is not —as some academics want to see it— a limited form of expression, inferior and preceding to writing but quite the contrary. The symbol is the undying way to simultaneously express a rational concept linked inseparably to an emotional image. Maximum wisdom. The ancient ones knew this from before we stopped feeling, from before the word 'science' existed. When a human being recovers equilibrium they go back to being sensitive to the power of these symbols; symbols talk.

Mexican ceramic seal

The symbol of the stairs and the spiral was not only found in South America but we also find it in Central and North

America. This is currently the symbol for the Quetzalcoatl priesthood. Many cultures of the Americas shared great symbols and understandings. I have heard all kinds of interpretations about it but the one I find truly transcendental is the one that understands the stairs as the representation of Space and the spiral as Time. Time and Space united in one symbol. Pachamama and Pachakamaq together. In the same way, in the north the Aztecs called their main deity Ometeo, combination of words that express measure and movement. They were obviously talking about the same thing; measure relates to space and movement to time.

Altar to Qorikancha

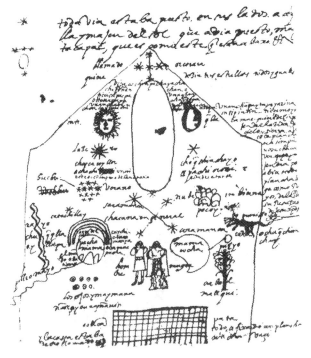

Representation of the main altar in the temple of Qorikancha in Cusco, according to the chronicles of Juan de Santa Cruz Pachacuti.

Following the same dualistic conception, after understanding the parity of all that exists once creation has been manifested, Tawantinsuyo wise ones deduced that after the original duality —Pachamama-Pachakamaq—, existed a series of levels through which these two energies descended and expressed themselves until they reached the human expression and manifested themselves in it, again, as the last duality: reason and feeling. The main altar found on the main temple in Cusco could not but reflect this: all levels of manifestation expressing themselves in the form of parities hierarchically organized. The feminine to the left and the masculine to the right. We are beings formed by these two energies that manifest in us as our feelings and our mind. We must recognize this and wonder what this concretely means in our life.

I do not feel the capacity to make any comment without falling into speculations about what these symbols meant over 500 years ago, but I do believe I can present some reflections that help meditate on some not so clear points in this diagram that I take as a valuable reference but I cannot accept as the true cosmology of Tawantinsuyo.

First thing is that —even assuming the impeccable intention of who attempted to transmit the information about this cosmology with absolute faithfulness— there exists the possibility that this document does not correspond exactly with reality. That is to say 100% of data transmitted does not coincide with the real altar found in Qorikancha before the invasion. Even though there is not an exact date for the chronicle that has this document, it is placed approximately 100 years after the destruction of the temple. This means that there is little possibility that the author observed the aforementioned altar with his own eyes. From this it is deduced that an older person passed on the information, which geometrically raises the possibilities of error, although involuntary.

One point of consensus about the empty and circular space — which was a disc of pure gold in the original altar— is to relate it to the great creator Wiraqocha to whom the chronicle teller calls 'the maker, the true Sun'. To leave a blank spot symbolizes the imperceptibility of its mystery. It is more than clear —at least in this drawing— that Wiraqocha represents unity since it is the only element without a counterpart inside the system of parities expressed in there. This fact reinforces vigorously our position that Wiraqocha is the neutral non-polarized principle and that it is a mistake to confuse it with the 'masculine' principle of Pachakamaq.

The next thing that raises my curiosity is that immediately after the great creator, the figures of the Sun and the Moon follow which also express a major duality but not the ultimate, as would Pachamama and Pachakamaq —which is absent—. The third thing is that we find a version of Pachamama very low in the hierarchy and on the masculine side. There is an interesting interpretation of this fact in the book Moon, Sun and Witches by the anthropologist Irene Silverblatt. She points that to put the greatest deity of most Andean ethnic groups —Pachamama in all its local versions— in a position of less importance could have been a strategy in the last stage of the Incan period to strengthen the dominant position and establish the solar origin of its dynasty.

Making a great effort to not fall into speculation, I leave everything with a question mark. I prefer to be prudent and even suspicious before daring to base the whole Andean cosmology on a document that is not first hand and which represents only the last part of what we call the Fourth Tawantinsuyo, the Incan time.

Unity and diversity

Lets remember for an instant our fractal example (page 22) of the segment that is divided in two, and then one of the halves is again divided in two and so on and so forth. Through this image we recognize these opposing and complementary energies that express two opposing codes or guidelines: one, to maintain the concept of unity in all of creation and as long as eternity lasts; and the other, to express diversity infinitely.

I relate the manifested unity with Time, Pachakamaq, the masculine principle; and diversity with Space, Pachamama, the feminine principle. However, I have wondered how and when the values change around when they touch the human sphere, since within us unity and feeling are naturally and spontaneously associated with the feminine and the rational and the mind with diversity and the masculine. I do not want to omit at this point that I felt really confused because the whole system of associations flows perfectly until it reaches the human being where the concepts are inverted. Maybe feeling is part of the masculine archetype and reason part of the feminine? All observations tell us the opposite. Woman assembles, brings together, searches for unity, family whereas man usually holds a much more individualistic position. Besides, it is evident that feeling unites and mind separates. When I thought everything was lost, all of a sudden I saw myself rescued from the jaws of conflict and dual logic and I remembered that I was writing about quadripartition. There had to be other ways to approach the impasse.

The mastery of the Ying Yang symbol explains this transformation of the principle of diversity of feminine in masculine better than one thousand words. Even the supposedly absolutes are subject to transformation processes, where after some time they definitely manifest the opposing nature. The white dot inside the black space will grow until it exactly inverts the proportion as well as the black dot in the white space will grow until it becomes the opposite. We also should not forget that they are both turning inside the circle, which will always make them occupy each other's place. What a paradox, they challenge us to achieve a sensitive mind and a wise feeling.

The ancient *I Ching* book or *Book of mutations* precisely studies the relationships between active and passive, masculine and feminine. When consulted as an oracle method it allows us to build a hexagram or set of six lines, where each line can be of four types and express four different energies that are also related to the following numeric values:

6 represents the line old ying

7 represents the line young yang

8 represents the line young ying

9 represents the line old yang

The 'pure' lines named old ying and old yang are called to become their opposites due to the tremendous internal tensions they represent. Old ying becomes young yang and old yang becomes young ying.

The mind

'How the minds turns into the color of life'.

The mind is not a demon to exorcise, a monster to be tamed, something to subdue. If we utilize it well it can also be seen as something beautiful, as a boundless source of creativity, imagination and poetry. What enslaves us turns into what liberates us and what liberates us turns into what enslaves us, including the mind, religions and spiritual paths. The mind is also a mechanism, a perception system. We cannot blame the manufacturer is we misuse the machine because we do not understand it.

Nowadays that most people know the basic functioning of a computer, it is easier to understand the human mind. The brain is the *hardware* —including neuronal networks— and the *software* is 'the way of thinking'. Each human being has unique and personalized *software*, in some case with very old versions. And others with the updated versions: and better not even talk about those that have viruses and do not realize it.

The mind is a fine and marvelous instrument but it needs some adjustments. We also have to consider —and this is part of its magical nature— that it has its own improving system. It should be known that it is optional, it activates through consciousness and will and it is not and it cannot be mechanical or automatic. Thus there cannot be a magical formula, a mechanical rite or *mantra* for evolution and self-knowledge. Each one has to adapt the teachings to his or her own reality.

For the most part we confuse the intellectual development of the mind with its evolution. We believe that 'life', our parents, school, society and university are sufficient to guarantee the complete development of our mind but this is not so. All these influences develop it only in part, in one way. That is to say towards the outside. But there is nothing or nobody in society that indicate that there is also a development towards the inside. You could be 60 years old, a great philosopher, a quantum physician or any other profession but your mind can continue to be that of a selfish child, incapable of seeing or accepting its own incoherence. Emotions drive you inside, they overflow you and you don't know what to do with your pain so you put it in a trunk, you burry it, you try to forget it and you learn to live only on the surface. But it will always be there waiting until you decide to accept it and heal it for good.

The mind is not just the monster that many religions teach, it is also a tender child, unprotected and almost abandoned by life, that learned by himself to bring food to his plate in the streets and could not develop all his potential as a human being. Ayahuasca showed me that child and I decided to raise him, protect him, teach him, understand him and love him. Understand my mind like it really was the mind of a child helped me greatly to understand myself and moreover, to understand others. Each day I became more tolerant in my perceptions because I saw all human beings in the different phases of the evolution of this child-mind.

I find it ridiculous to judge the behavior of someone that is exactly at the phase of their evolution; as much as judging my two-year-old daughter when she answers the phone —she does her best—. In any case it would be a problem if she continued to behave in the same manner when she is 30 years old. And that is mostly what happens to us.

At his moment I remember the words 'son of man'. What was he trying to tell us? Is it maybe the son of mind? That who reduces his own mind? The word 'Christ' comes from Greek and shares the same root as the word 'crystal'. According to a tradition, Christ was not a name but a title, a level some people reached. This might mean that the title of Christ was given to those that came to be 'crystalline', the transparency of the mind. We perceive part of reality through our mind. If we see the mind as a crystal through which we see reality, each human being has a crystal personally stained and with different degrees of distortion regarding 'reality'. Thus it is useless to try to convince someone to see things the way we see them. Each being sees their stained and distorted reality same as we see ours. Even those that believe they are 'illuminated masters' see their relatively stained and distorted reality. It is all about degrees and levels. What you see, you see. What you don't see, you don't see. And what you don't see, does it even exist?

But we cannot resign and leave things as they are. It would be good if each one of us starts cleaning the window through which we look at life and not look at how dirty your neighbor's windows are. Maybe one day we see more or less the same. It would be amusing to know if we are actually watching the same movie. Each one is to clean their own crystal.

In a curious manner, the mind works in many ways like the crystals. One of the proprieties of our mind is the capability of separating and splitting the only reality in its different elements. As the prism splits light in its seven colors, our mind has that capacity called analytical that allows us to split everything, analyze its parts and continue doing it as much as possible. These times we live in are a perfect example of analysis and specialization. We have achieved such a level of specialization in professions that sometimes it makes communication between two people of different specializations very difficult. I am not against specialization or analysis as long as we are conscious of the opposing and complementary process, which is synthesis.

We need to take a great leap in our mind as humanity and not just individually in the same way it has been happening since the beginning of time. Take the leap into simultaneity in a collective manner. We must develop analytical thinking but also synthetic thinking, we must have the capacity to observe reality from 'outside' but also observe the 'inner' reality. We must develop thought but also love. The human being is reason and feeling.

I sincerely believe that the image of the mind as a crystal is one of the best analogies to describe it. Imagine you are a child again and you come close to one of those shop windows full of beautiful objects. You come very close to the window in order to see better and so you can be closer to those things you so want, so you end up squishing your nose against the glass like children usually do. Reality is very similar. You are the child and the big crystal is your mind. When you are fully touching the glass —the mind— you can see the objects very clearly and for a moment you forget the glass is even there. If you are totally identified with the mind, you don't recognize its existence or its limits. But if you take a little distance, you not only continue to see the objects behind the glass, but you see the glass and the objects also; and if you take one more step back, you don't just see the glass and the objects but you start to see your own reflection —your true self— and everything behind you. The moment when you can see the objects, the glass, your own reflection and what is behind is what some call illumination. I prefer to use the words 'to be awake' or 'conscious'. All this work aims to make resonate in you the desire to be conscious, what many of us call *awaken the witness*. The first step is to recognize that the mind is part of me but I am not only the mind.

In the times of our Cro-Magnon ancestors, the chief was not necessarily the wisest one or the one with better ideas. For the most part he was a big guy with a powerful arm capable of lifting a heavy club that could squash in one blow the ideas and the head of his opponents. That is how the first pattern of leadership might have been established. Not only did you have to have a good idea but also the means to make it prevail. For reasons inherent to our species, males are generally slightly bigger and stronger than females. Because of this, the same caveman pattern has been reproduced over and over until it arrived in our homes nowadays and many cultures and societies were forged between then and now, evidently including religions.

The feeling

The proposal related to the basic duality expressed in human beings through the mind and the heart or reason and feeling needs to seek broad consensus to share the redefinition of some important words, because they are the foundation of this new vision of the Fifth Tawantinsuyo. The first word I propose to redefine and specify is the word *feeling*.

It is necessary to finish reading these pages to be able to understand the overall sketch of what they attempt to communicate before questioning it. The *feeling* for me is *the feeling*. This means it is not two or three or four but *the* feeling, unique and sacred. And it can only be defined by the word love that at the same time represents the archetype of unity. It is invariably present in the heart of everything that exists.

This feeling-love is the perfect expression of the love of who designed and created all manifestation. It was placed in the heart of all beings like the greatest gift a father and a mother can give to their children: a piece of themselves so we can communicate, so we can find ourselves, so we remember that in essence we are all the same; that in unity we are all the same. This is the key through which we can recognize ourselves in equality.

The basic unit divides itself in two parts. One continues to represent unity and the other represents duality. In this vision supported by tradition, the heart is related to unity and in correspondence with the other attributes of this part of duality, it is also related to immutability. Thus love is unique and has not changed since the beginning of creation. The same love with which everything was created was always present in the heart of the first man and the first woman that walked this earth and it is exactly the same love that is in your heart and mine. There is no difference between one love and another, there are no 'qualities' of love. Love is unique and unconditional. You either feel it or you don't.

What happens with everything else we thought were 'feelings'? According to this approach everything else are emotions and they are in the mind. This does not mean they are necessarily good or bad, or that they are to be belittled. Emotions come in all types, in different intensities and they are part of our reality.

To reach a good understanding of the redefinition of the word 'feeling' seems to me fundamental to achieve greater understandings. It is important to free it from all negative connotations like it is given in everyday use. Stop saying 'I feel sad' or 'I feel angry', or even 'I feel happy'. This understanding suggests that I do not feel any of those things and I only feel love. What we should say is 'I have sadness in my mind' or 'I have thoughts of anger or jealousy' or simply 'I am happy'. The feeling will always be one, pure, endless, indestructible, immutable and eternal within the heart of each being. Whereas emotions of the mind are the expression of diversity, always plentiful, always changing. They could be positive and sometimes negative; we do not judge them, we only observe them as a reality so we can change them when things are clear enough.

Now we can continue the conversation, we have a great thing in common: my feeling is exactly the same as yours, you love as much as I do, our difference does not lie in our feeling but in our mind. And this difference does not have to be an insurmountable barrier between us. On the contrary, it is the opportunity to dare contemplate together, celebrate and honor the mystery in life that is the diversity expressed in our differences. This always was, is and will be the essence of Tawantinsuyo.

My mind does not have hatred towards those who do not believe what I believe. To hate somebody for thinking different seems to be a frequent problem for those that do not clearly see what unites us and what separates us. Because of that, I do not pretend to convince anybody, I just display mi proposal like a carpet before your feet. If it works for you, use it.

The mental pattern that makes us have hatred, or at least, that we don't appreciate those that have ideas contrary to ours is frequently used, particularly around politics or religion. At some point all of us have seen from family members to entire countries confronting and even destroying each other over these subjects. Our beliefs should not separate us so much. This is one clear piece of evidence of how the religious does not live in the heart but in the mind. The mind can produce very intense emotions of devotion and 'mystical experiences' but when you touch 'its beliefs', period, no more dialog, war starts. My brother becomes my enemy

The word 'religion' is one that has suffered greatest changes in meaning. Now we call religions to some political movements with a 'humanist' basis. Religion —from the root religar, re unite— is very far form achieving that objective. More and more it is a cause of separation and distancing. I am not saying having beliefs is bad, nor religion —a form to re unite—. Beliefs are also beautiful and it is perfect that each one has their own and gathers in groups according to affinities. But we cannot ignore the damage created by intolerance or the abuse —of those supported by economic powers— making great efforts to destroy diversity. When we become conscious that what unites us is something so great, our differences could look insignificant. A trap we should avoid is when in the heat of defending our beliefs, our minds become insensitive, dogmatic, out of control, fanatic, incapable of perceiving our own heart, our own love and the damage that we can cause others.

Another wonderful gift that branches off the vision of the unique feeling is that it becomes much easier to understand and forgive people that in their ignorance do deplorable actions. If we assume that within the heart of each human being lies the sacred spark of the same love —the great love that grants us all our sacredness— and if we accept that in the diversity of our minds that any mind (by confusion or ignorance, permanent or temporary) can have thoughts that in the end hurt one or many human beings, it will be much easier to understand them and even forgive them. Because according to this vision, even the most evil of men deserves to be forgiven because his heart is in essence the same as ours. The difference is that his mind chose the wrong paths.

Mind and heart are the ultimate expression of the primordial energies, the great duality that we will continue to investigate in all its manifestations.

Including logic

The problem is in the type of logic we use. I call *dual excluding logic* to that that was taught to us like it was the pinnacle of human evolution. It is based in that if there are two contrary proposals, if one is true the other one necessarily has to be false. Example: 'There is one true God. If my God is true, therefore your God is false'. This type of logic does not allow the two proposals to be true. 'If I am right and you disagree then you are not right'. We are not saying that this logic system is bad or incorrect but simply that it is not the only one and it cannot be applied to every situation. There are other logic systems that must be learned and used in different cases.

It is absurd to apply this dual logic to every case when we only perceive a partial and subjective reality. The ancient sages found that the most complete vision of reality is one that includes all possible points of view, not only those we like or find convenient. But particularly the opposing ones. They called this *including logic*. 'If I am right, you can also be right. Therefore we can both be right'. This type of logic goes beyond duality, it truly resolves it in a positive harmonious way and it transcends dialectics and places us just one step from understanding *quadripartition*, the *Tawantinsuyo*.

Dual logic inappropriately used is destructive, it confronts one position with another until one erodes and the other prevails. Including logic creates a dynamic equilibrium where a consensus exit has to be found, an alternated predominance: 'now you, then me'. This impedes the useless wasting of energies and promotes maximum benefit to both parties. What it is important to know is in which field to apply each of these systems. There are simple things that get resolved easily with excluding logic, countless activities of everyday life (buying, selling, building). But there are other more complex ones like human relations or perceptions of reality for which we need a more appropriate, non-excluding system.

Spirit and matter

I write in between my two-year-old daughter requests to help her dress her doll. I will put down my pen as many times as necessary because what she is doing is as sacred as what I am doing, and 'mine' is not more important than 'hers'. One of the great distortions of reality was to oppose in an irreconcilable and antagonistic way 'spirit' and 'matter'. Evidently using dual logic. This is also part of the skillful work of some shady hand that goes around altering divine scriptures.

The 'spiritualists' teach us that there is a material reality that is temporary and another spiritual reality that is eternal; that we must get rid of our materiality in order to elevate to the regions of the spirit; that we must renounce and detach from our material and 'mundane' activities and transcend them so we can dedicate ourselves to spiritual matters: ceremonies, meditations, prayers, those spiritual things. In this discourse I see —in the best of cases— nothing more than the naïve continuity of our Cro-Magnon ancestors. It still expresses the belief in the superiority of one gender and pretends to continue to take advantage of a naïve and natural association of the spiritual with male and the material with female.

The relation is not wrong in itself, what is wrong is the interpretation. In pre-Columbian America, wise ones did not put down women —the concept of parity was very clear— and this association matter-*mater*-mother-woman would not have caused any scandals. I insist, the problem is not in that relation — spirit-male, matter-female— but in the value that kind religions smuggled and sold us. If we teach that spirit is the elevated, the sublime and that matter is the contrary —with all the polarized adjectival charges of each case— we are sending many messages to the subconscious that besides being false, they bring a lot of damage to both genders. We do not lift the club any more to squash discrepancies. We learned to lift culture, education and even religion to do the same, that is to say, to 'put women in their place', matter. From these humble pages we pretend to start a revolution of love, of recognizing and of respect. A revolution that both matter and women have been waiting for since the beginning of humanity.

Returning again the idea of the change of axis, I want to also relate it with an essential paradigmatic change for these times. The classic vision of spirit-matter was always considered an opposition. It can be expressed graphically in this manner through a vertical axis. The spirit is the elevated and in a pejorative sense, matter is the mundane.

Spirit

Matter

Ancient knowledge sets out to modify this vision moving from the vertical axis to the horizontal, observing them not in opposition but in complementarity:

Spirit  Matter

A creating principle exists previous to any manifestation. This maker of a neutral gender suddenly got polarized and became masculine–Lord God, Our Father; and the mother? Where did our mother end up? Who would dare make the feminine archetype disappear from the sacred trinity? I will address this in the third chapter.

This is the breaking point for me: do we believe religions are a creation of men or of the great maker? Honestly, for me they are human creations and thus fallible and perfectible. I am not saying they are bad in themselves but that they are simply human, with all the vices and virtues that adorn any person. But they should recognize a little bit that they ought to change according to necessity in spite of waiting someone that will fix it all every 2000 years.

It is very difficult for me to explain this exclusion of the sacred dimension that women, the feminine and matter suffered. We could try to understand it in terms of the incipient mental evolution of the ancient Judeo-Christian people, but unfortunately there is something else. There is a hidden and stubborn intention to continue in this way. The rage of this patriarchal doctrine towards these peoples and cultures that maintained the original equilibrium is not casual and it is very meaningful. A very similar phenomenon took place first in Europe through the witch-hunt. Pure coincidence? It is effortless for me to see the divine and sacred in the wife, daughters, mother, girlfriends, mountains, earth, planet and finally in the heart.

The heart is as sacred as the mind, since they both are the last terminals where this sacred duality we call Pachamama and Pachakamaq are expressed. Now it is a little easier to understand why our relationship with the planet is how it is. As long as we follow the wrong associations —spirit-masculine-elevated, matter-feminine-profane— we will continue treating the planet and the woman not as a mother but as a thing.

The feminine has been denigrated a lot and with much hypocrisy, in spite of this some religions managed to make many women accept this political and religious order and even renounce to many essential aspects of their femininity to continue to exist and compete in the present economic system.

Some years ago in a ceremony, a friend approached me and said to me: 'what a beautiful prayer you said in defense of women'. I told her I did not say any prayer in defense of women, women know how to defend themselves. The condition of the abused is as disgraceful as that of the abuser. As a sacred man I pray for the dignity of women and men. The need to correct this dreadful imbalance becomes more and more urgent. And to remain silent would make us as responsible as those committing the injustice.

In the last few decades it has been seen how millions of people abandon formal religions and find new 'spiritual' paths. I find this good but the majority of them follow the old format, the ancient paradigm —spirit-masculine, matter-feminine— and they are only valid as a new step, a bridge towards something ever more real.

I know many people involved in this 'spiritual activities', courses, workshops, meditations and ceremonies. Many come to my house to spend some time. In the mornings we talk about very 'elevated' subjects while my wife prepares lunch for everybody. Lunch ends, I get up to wash dishes and they remain talking about spiritual things. This is what I am referring to, this is the best image I can offer of 'spiritual' people disconnected from the 'material'. This has happened many times and a few times someone realized, got up from the table and told me with a 'I got it' smile: 'leave it, I will do the dishes'. To disdain 'material' activities because they are considered mundane, trivial or little elevated, or to not consider important and sacred ceremonies the daily preparation of food, doing laundry or spending hours tending to, playing with and raising our children is a sign of little understanding and it is the first thing we must change.

I also remember the story of a friend that many years ago, he was in search of 'spiritual realization' and he spent hours in the morning meditating and singing *mantras*, completely avoiding to help in other activities. One day at lunchtime he sat at his usual spot at the table. He saw his wife sit down at the table with a steaming delicious plate of spaghettis and she started eating. He waited looking at his empty plate until he couldn't hold it any more and asked: what about me? His wife replied: 'for you dear, I prepared a very special plate: I put four hundred *Oms*, one hundred and eight *Gayatris* and twenty five Our fathers. Enjoy'.

They brain washed us for thousand of years believing that we must seek the spiritual and reject the material and it is not so. We must recognize the sacredness of existence in both. Ancient and wise religions like Hinduism have been distorted to the point of transmitting teachings contrary to their essential truth. The best example we can find is yoga. Many people assume that people that practice yoga are dedicating to something solely spiritual. But the root of the word 'yoga' is in the word 'yugo' and in this case it means 'union'. Union not just between creator and creation but also between spirit and matter. The proof of this is they developed a series of exercises to maintain health and to become conscious of the importance of the body. The perfect equilibrium between spirit and matter.

They ask me if I follow a spiritual path. The answer is obviously no. I follow a very ancient sacred path of integration between the material and the spiritual. Where does it start? In recognizing the sacredness in both parts of duality: Pachamama and Pachakamaq, the Sun and the Moon, Heaven and Earth, Time and Space, my father and my mother, my mind and my heart. We have to start understanding which are the facets of each one, those of the masculine principle and those of the feminine. Then we have to understand which are the distortions of each one, how the imbalance comes to be, the excess of either of them. We are a mixture of these two energies. In their pure state, they must be mixed in equal parts, but this is not always so. Life demands that one of the energies prevails at times and then the other. We must always return to equilibrium. We cannot build a healthy world based on the predominance of one of these manifestations.

Reality

'Reality is the path to heaven,
not the freedom you take with your hands
but the one you reach when you let go of your ideas'
Vasco Masías

Let us observe our reality for a few moments. We could be laying in bed reading, in our favorite sofa, in an airport seat or in a wonderful place called nature. We normally call reality to everything that we see around us at that moment. But how many of us include inner reality in the greater reality? In other words, how many of us give the inner world the status of reality? Are our thoughts real or temporary states not connected among them and they do not affect external reality nor interact with it? It would seem that for the majority of people, the intensity and type of emotions we experiment would not be important enough to consider them part of reality. They taught us that reality is what we perceive and in a certain sense they are right because we never 'see' our inner reality, we do not even consider it. It does not exist for many. So if we do not take into account the latter, in the best of cases all we can perceive is but 50% of the total reality. Again we find ourselves before a beautiful duality: within and without. Is this separation real? Yes and no.

Many times I clearly saw how this supposed separation between internal and external realities appeared complemented by something we could call *the threshold*. The threshold of a door or a window is that small place in between two spaces that is neither inside or outside. We can easily relate it with the witness, consciousness. When I perceive what is inside as part of me and at the same time I perceive all that is outside also as part of me and I perceive that who perceives, at this moment I am contemplating the mystery of quadripartition.

Faced with the subject of reality, the majority of eastern 'spiritual' traditions tell us that this world is pure illusion and the 'true' reality is that of the spirit; that when we die, true life actually starts. The version of the western believer is not very different: 'Behave well, do what I say and you will almost freely enjoy eternal life'. Both versions dismiss the very important moment of living *here and now*, assigning it a relative and secondary importance. I find a serious lack of respect towards the creators to dismiss the greatest gift they have given us: life in this planet.

With relation to the question of what happens after death, some pretend to place our 'eternal life and joy' in the hands of spiritual intermediaries that, even though they do not attribute themselves the power to decide who will be saved and who will not be saved, they like to make forecasts. In addition I think that offering eternal life is a non creative solution to resolve the drama of human existence. Whatever the *post mortem* truth is, the attitude of diminishing this reality of here and now by calling it illusion or temporary truth hides a bit of cowardness. It aims to move human emotions like fear, insecurity, uncertainty and attachment with the goal to put pressure and even blackmail emotionally. To consider that life is a simple 'illusion', the amazing and highly intense experience that is virtually all we have is somewhere between comic and humiliating in my view. I will not let them rob me of the right of joy in each tear of this sacred 'illusion'. I will live this life with all the honor and respect it deserves as if it was the only one (because it might as well be the only one) thanking all the love and pain that my days bring. And when this time is over, we will occupy ourselves with 'other realities', but only when I reach them. I do not want to speculate whereas they will be more or less real.

All the ancient spiritual teaching continue to frame things from the point of view of confrontation, the non resolved duality spirit-matter. Is this life real or pure illusion? Does internal reality exist or only the external one? Do inside and outside exist? Am I just spirit or pure matter? The answer in these cases will definitely be: yes and no, regardless that it will bother many. These subjects cannot be dealt with the dual logic we are used to. For materialists, what we see is all that is real whereas for spiritualists this is pure illusion: for me both are trapped in their respective extremes of the pendulum, unable to imagine an opposing and complementary reality and even less a simultaneous one.

How much can we perceive this reality we call God or this God we call reality? The truth is that it is defined by what I call *consciousness*. Simply: what are you capable of realizing? A group of people that do not have internal reality very clear dare — supported by their financial power through media— to impose a reality and disqualify other realities. This becomes a means of control and illusionary power. Those that impose 'reality' spend enormous fortunes spreading something arbitrary. And even then it will be only a part of the greater reality. We will always have the power over our internal reality and no one but ourselves can have that control if we do not allow it.

In our times, we call reality what people believe in. If many believe in the same thing or they repeat the same story, it becomes real for them. This is how different groups plant many ideas. Spread through media and believed by multitudes. The paradox of all this is that what you believe in becomes real for you. Right or wrong. God is as real for Christians as Vishnu for Hindus, Ala for Muslims and Brahman for Buddhists. With their respective heavens, hells, worlds, hierarchies and structures. I do not deny any of these realities, I consider them all. I believe them all to be true within an including reality. But it is not about to simply say that they are the same with different names. They are different gods and they all exist and are real, and each one of them creates and rules their own universe within this *multiverse* that is all of creation. It would of course be a mortal offense for many to not believe that their god is the only true one, for me they are all true and respectable. The final reality, the 'true god' is far beyond any attempt of separation. Why do we have to see things in this way? Why does my vision have to be radically opposed to the view of my brother to the extreme of becoming enemies? Even if all this happens in the realm of ideas, inside my mind?

On the other hand, reality is also the great fountain of true power, the fountain of endless love and energy. The more crystalline your mind becomes the clearer you will see and the easier it will be to nurture yourself with true energy that will allow to do or not do certain things. On the contrary, the more you dishonor your mind to accommodate it to your interests and the deeper you sink in this self-deceit game, the weaker you will get and blind random forces will rule your life diving you in a sea of contradictions. Again I insist: there is no more God than reality or more reality than God.

A journey within

Lets imagine ourselves as an energy sphere and represent its center with a dot having the opposite color than the outline. In order to brake the pattern white=good, black=bad we will choose red and blue. Red at the center and after a delicate and almost imperceptible gradient we reach a beautiful sky blue. Lets relate our heart, our feeling to the red nucleus, tiny as an atom made of the purest red located in what we will call *the depth of our being*. The millions and trillions of different atoms —from this nucleus until we reach the surface— are the diversity, our mind or our reason. There exist not only two realities or elements —the center and the surface, the deep and the superficial— but a third reality exists: relation, consciousness, movement. It has many names, it depends on each moment. This relation between our depth and our surface, our heart and our mind will determine many things.

Let us for a moment observe our sphere and imagine that a particle enters into it —it could be an event, an experience or a perception— to be known by the mind. Then it continues its path towards our depth to be loved by our feeling and later it returns to the surface. It leaves a footprint behind in every atom it touched. These modified atoms contain our memories that can be more or less pleasant, happy or painful. And also more or less profound. Let us say that they are placed in different levels according to their intensity. After a decade we have a good amount of memories, some very happy and some painful.

All this happens within us, in a place that we can barely perceive because our mind has never been educated to look within. When several decades have passed we are so full of painful memories in our depth that the mind is less and less interested to know what happens within. It condemns us to live superficially. True happiness will very much depend on facing all our pending issues that almost in their totality are related with forgiveness: to forgive any harm done to us or to forgive ourselves for something we did or did not do. We will first have to dissolve many mental patterns fed by negative emotions —like hatred, pride or resentment— to be able to forgive. It is very difficult to not hate someone that has done much harm to us. Hatred is a very powerful mental pattern. Furthermore, our reason —our mind— could even say that not only it is reasonable but also just to hate those that harm us. But the problem is not whether we are capable or forgiving or not at that moment, but to know that the pattern of hatred has to be dissolved. The point of the matter is to know which direction we have to take to dissolve the pattern some day. It does not matter if we are not able to do that right now. For a person that is calm, peacefully reading it can be very easy to say 'I can do this, I don't hate anyone'. But what would happen if all of a sudden that person was a victim of a great injustice or aggression? Would they be up to the task? I think the answer would change because dissolving the pattern of hatred is a characteristic of an awakened being. Each level brings trials and I beg you, do not ask for them because they will come at their own time.

If we see the heart as unity —immutable reality— and the mind as diversity —the opposite, absolute variability— I find that I cannot change the immutable. My love was and will always be, but I can change my mind. It is just a matter of trying. What is the first thing we will ask our mind? Flexibility and willingness to change.

Let us imagine our sphere again. This particle that enters our life and heads towards the heart to be touched by our love chooses one of our mental atoms as a companion in this long path towards the nucleus. But we need brave thoughts capable to risk everything in this journey of transformation. Each atom of our mind that accompanies each particle of perception is transformed as they approach the heart. It becomes a bit more *sensitive*. Thus, different from many 'spiritual' schools that consider the mind as an enemy to be destroyed, I see it as my best friend, my best tool, my best resource, as a system of creativity and of imagination almost infinite. We can create a reality so beautiful and elevated that paradise would seem boring and dull. The mind is not to be feared or destroyed, it is to be reeducated. It was the mind of man that created divine spaces filled with music and poetry or horrible images like hell and its eternal fire. The mind will always be a simple tool, it all depends on what use you give it.

Simultaneity

Look at the worm that eats the leaf.
Look at the leaf hanging from the tree.
Look at the tree that grows in the woods.
Look at the woods adorning the earth.
Look at the earth turning in the cosmos.
Look at the cosmos sustaining life.
Look at life in the worm that eats the leaf.

When we see the worm we don't see the leaf, when we see the leaf we don't see the tree, when we see the tree...and so on and so forth. Our mind can't see more than one thing at a time. Immediately after focusing on something we stop seeing the rest. How do we manage to see the worm, the cosmos and life all at once? If we concentrate in the cosmos, why can't we see the woods or even less the worm? Why do we get lost in the step from the general to the particular and vice versa? Why do we loose perspective?

It is all a matter of work and training, but we have to be clear about where to start. Therefore life laid the path for us in this way: to go from the absolutist dictatorship of the mind towards a simultaneous contemplation of two realities —mind and heart, the unity of feeling and the diversity of reason— to later see the third, the relation, the consciousness; and then the fourth dimension, the fifth, etc. At the end, to see life in the worm that eats the leaf. It is just a matter of training and of wanting to change our mind, accustom it to search the diametrically opposed thinking to the one offered to us at first sight. When we see a bonfire, why do we just see the warmth and the life that the fire gives us? Why do we not see the life of the tree that goes burning? May our mind be conscious of its own reality and the reality of its closest neighbor, the heart.

The relation

If we conceive our mind as the masculine part —the husband— and our heart as the feminine part —the wife— what kind of couple are we? Does our mind scream, imposes itself, does whatever it wants and our heart weeps in silence, hangs in there and waits until one day things get better? We all have more or less the same beginning. How do we begin to improve and heal this relationship? Knowing our heart and our mind, our feminine and our masculine analyzing first how these energies are in their pure state, meditating about it.

The masculine principle is the energy that is expansive, initial, explosive, centrifugal, analytical, active, emitting. The feminine is the energy that concentrates, sustains, it is centripetal, synthetic, passive, receptive. So this can be understood, I implore to not make judgments about the value of the qualities of duality as active=positive=good and passive=negative=bad. Being active is not good or bad; it all depends on the moment and circumstances. Sometimes it will be the right thing and sometimes catastrophic. Besides, we are talking about archetypical qualities and not of the naïve and temporary identification each person has with their gender.

The most frequent distortion of masculine energy lies in its expansive quality. When does this energy express negatively? When it is incapable of determining its own limit, when it ignores how it affects its surroundings. It then perverts itself and goes from being expansive to being invasive. That is where problems start, disequilibrium. This is evident in the current civilization.

Weather you are a man or a woman, how do you determine when the expansive energy becomes invasive? We arrive again at the point of simultaneity. How to sustain two aspects in our consciousness, two realities that are sometimes distant or contradictory? In the actual case of our expansive energy it is about accompanying this expansion and at the same time realize when we start to invade both others and the space of our own heart. The relationship between our heart and our mind is the primordial relationship. If we do not get to understand it and have at least an acceptable bond within ourselves, I very much doubt that we can have a good bond with other people. If our mind is capable of misleading us, how can we not mislead others?

We effortlessly see in the world that relationships are mostly disastrous, particularly couples. We take for granted that being in love is enough to have a good bond but it is not so. The falling in love is a mechanism to protect life which activates glands that segregate hormones that make us see everything wonderful. I would call it a kind of emotional drunkenness. Every defect and weakness of our partner appears understandable and some even beautiful. After some time this passes and the relationship is seen the way it really is. Without this little help from nature, our continuity would be almost utopian. After several months we see things clearer and we get scared. It does not make a difference if we were mislead or we misled the other, the point is that we have a relationship in our plate. We do not really know how we arrived at it and we will resolve it according to the type of conditioning that we have. If we are the type that likes to suffer, we will hold on to it even if it is the most inadequate one and it makes us unhappy for the rest of our life. If we are the selfish kind we will not give it a chance and at the first chance we will either break it or consolidate our dominant position, we will be the one setting the rules.

To start a relationship is very easy. However it is very difficult to know how to end it. Once the 'inloveness' is over, if the couple has a future they can start to work it in the path of love. If it does not have a future sometimes we insist on a bond that is harmful for both parties, out of weakness, confusion, need or whatever. When we are not sufficiently satisfied with a relationship and we do not have the maturity to end it, we often fight each other gradually more violently, trying to obtain the necessary energy for separation from anger or rage, turning the end into a true hell. If we are not capable to accept the other person exactly as they are knowing that there will always be good and bad moments. Let us not search in violence the strength to end the relationship, but in love. 'I distance myself from this person because I love them and I don't want to keep ruining their life'. There is not such thing as a bad one and a good one in a relationship, human beings are like flavors or colors. There are good and bad combinations among people. Couple relationships are the best initiation school in these times.

Just as couple relationships are in *Kay pacha* —this world— the relationship between our mind and our heart is in our inner world, it belongs to what we call *Uhu pacha*. The work in this field starts by understanding that only in the sincerity of our inner space can me achieve a model of relationship free of conditionings. If I succeed to establish in myself a loving, honest relationship between my masculine and my feminine parts, I will learn a lot about relationships in general and of what I can or cannot expect from my counterpart in the second level, this world —*Kay pacha*—. For a relationship to work, both parties have to have the capacity to put themselves in each others shoes and be able to see things from the opposite side. And this wonderful opportunity will always be within us, each time we are capable of going beyond the identification with our bodies gender and understand that duality, polarity and relationship are also within us and at that point we will have the opportunity to experiment how the other part feels.

When we are capable to reeducate our mind, refine it, make it a little more 'sensitive', learn to turn down the volume of those screeching or passionate screams, when all that noise is turned down it is not difficult to start listening to the subtle voice of the heart that simply says: love. In each pulse it is saying 'love'. Both a new chapter of life and a great challenge for the mind start here because it is easier to govern in an abusive way than in consensus. Once this voice has been heard it is very difficult to live ignoring it. At this point the mind asks itself: 'how would love be?'

Here we have again the problem of the meaning of words. What our heart calls love is something our mind does not know exactly. It has similar emotions but it does not exactly know love. It knows attachment, desire, jealousy, missing, tenderness and it is even capable of inventing its own category: mental love. True, unconditional love is the one feeling and we have to differentiate it from the rest of emotions that are in the mind. At this point each mind starts its long path to learn what love is.

Energy and form

I have always heard that energy defines form. I seriously asked myself a few years ago: 'is this true? Would not form define energy?' My answer was: 'to say the former is as arbitrary as the latter'. For these two sentences to become true we would only have to add 'sometimes'. Sometimes energy defines form; sometimes form defines energy. But the relationship between form and energy is much more complex and it is not only about which defines which.

Let us again escape from any absurd confrontations in order to know the truth. Lets get out of the dual logic and excluding thinking in order to enter a new understanding. When the ancient sages related the mental with the head and the feeling with the heart, they were showing off an extremely fine intuition. Thousands of years before it occurred to someone to explore and know the shape of the organs, the ancient ones more than understood that relationship.

Mind is mostly related to duality. If we look at the shape of the brain —where it lives— the first thing we observe is that it is formed by two halves, two hemispheres, one rational and another intuitive, artistic, emotive. In the same way, when a connection was established between the feeling and the heart, no one knew the internal shape of this organ that clearly shows four regions, four directions: left auricle, right auricle, left ventricle and right ventricle.

Number 4 contains 1, 2, 3 and 4. According to the ancient math of Pythagoras, the occult meaning of a number is obtained adding all the numbers that conform it: $4=1+2+3+4=10$, $10=1+0=1$. This means 4 also means unity. The heart is unity and the quaternary is unity. Did the energy of feeling want to inhabit our chest and give that shape to our main organ, or was the shape of this organ what allowed this energy to inhabit it?

It happened to me in three occasions that when I start learning rituals from a tradition, I looked —like a child amazed by form— for the formula that opened the door to other states of consciousness in order to obtain magical understandings. I observed carefully each gesture, each word and even each date of every action. I dreamed with discovering the secret of the ritual. On one hand this always ended up in disappointment and on the other hand I felt strengthened, convinced that no ritual of this or that culture could be the formula that opened the doors and that the mere personal capacity of penetrating into the mystery could achieve it: enter as a beam of light in the middle of the depth of the secret and discover that the ritual is not what you do but how you do it. Do you really know what you are doing or is it mere mimicking? Even though at the beginning a way of learning is imitation, when do you stop being an imitator and become a facilitator? If the purpose is pure and you have the will to persist you will soon realize that the secret is in the relationship you have with what you are doing and that is something that cannot be faked. It depends partially on how much tenderness and effort you have dedicated to what you do, not just to understanding the formula —the external— but to relate correctly with the essence. We always repeat the same pattern seeking to dominate the form to manage each situation. Three times were enough for me to learn. The form can be beautiful and very attractive but it is nothing without the essence.

I learned many things from the traditions of the ancient peoples of the Americas but I also found many inaccuracies, superstitions, and even false things. With time certain teachings have been so distorted that in some cases they have become lies. It is necessary to be very attentive to find the true teaching beyond all form. Even so, I still believe it is possible to find a lot of wisdom in ancient traditions.

This is a good moment to place a request to all those interested in ceremonies and traditions of the ancient peoples of the Americas. Since thousands of years ago, in many rituals done throughout the American continent, hides and feathers of different animals were used to 'connect' to the power and energy of these beings. Up until a few decades ago the hunting of these animals was done in a sacred way, i.e. in an honorable way, with a very pure intention and praying a lot for the animal to be sacrificed. In those times, many of these animals were not in the extreme danger of extinction that they are nowadays.

The reality nowadays is that many followers of modern shamanic schools do not stop even for a second to consider the utter damage they are causing to these beings of power, because when they buy their feathers or hides the only thing they are doing is supporting illegal pouching. The black market of shamanic objects dares to ignore this due to how profitable these sales are in the 'shamanshops'. Poor naïve, badly oriented people buy condor or eagle feathers, otorongos —Amazonian jaguar— and snakes to gift each other and decorate their temples and ceremonies without knowing that the only thing they are taking is animal remains. A condor feather can cost up to 10 US dollars here in Cusco. Can you imagine the price for a dead condor in the black market? Do you have any idea how many otorongos are left in the jungle? Without doubt, not many; probably a few hundred. Each hide and each feather we buy or that is gifted to us is part of this madness, of this extermination, of this circus of appearances. How can there be power in ignorance, in unconsciousness or in vanity? Is the power in the feather or skin of these brothers and sisters or rather in the love and respect we have for them? How easy it is to stay in the form and forget the energy. The power of these animals will come to us when we learn to love them, respect them, defend them, protect them and honor them, particularly when they are alive.

Truth and honesty

If I had to sum up all of the above in two pieces of advice, those would be love the truth and maintain honesty. Love the truth because it is the final goal, to enjoy seeing things exactly as they are; and to love honesty so that our mind does not change, distort or hide that truth. Always have truth as the most precious treasure and honesty as its best ally. Due to the weight of our conditionings, one cannot be honest 100% of the time in 100% of our relationships. The mechanical patterns of thinking make us lie over and over again creating great confusion. However, almost no person who considers themselves normal accept that they lie. Generally we are so asleep that we do not realize when we lie and we have the self-image of being honest and truthful. But this is not so, we are pathological liars, we lie to ourselves and to half of the world.

We mistake the intellectual development of our mind with our true evolution. Up to a certain part of the path they can certainly be parallel but it reaches a point where they follow opposite paths. Our mind develops such a capacity for argumentation that can turn any discussion almost infinite. The mind achieves word skills that can change any situation or discourse almost confusing us. I have met true jugglers of words capable of making any monstrosity seem as the most natural thing. We can only be saved form this kind of liars by our intuition and our love of truth.

The first step to be honest is to become aware of our lies, of all that mechanical part and our conditionings that make us act in that way. Because of this, couple relationships are a great opportunity to start the path of freedom practicing honesty. Once we decide to be honest with ourselves, the next step is to be honest with someone else, someone we fully trust that will not take advantage of our sincerity to hurt us, someone that helps us dissolve and overcome the conditionings that make us lie. One cannot be suddenly honest with the whole world all of the time. We can try but I don't think it is either efficient or real. The commitment has to start by being honest with one person all the time, whatever happens, whatever the cost. This is not a 'moral' question but a real one, it does not depend on the agreement or the rules each couple or each society have. Regardless of what the rules were, an agreement with someone should not be broken unilaterally nor should we make our partner believe the rules are being respected. It is very naïve and arrogant to think we are so smart that we can lie eternally without being caught. Truth and honesty are treasures that grow geometrically with time. Of course it is good to be honest *sometimes*, but this does not compare with the satisfaction to observe how day by day, year after year that relationship grows uncontaminated by lies and distrust, and how love and trust are potentialized thanks to continuity. And if we fail? Nothing happens, we ask for forgiveness and we start again, humbly and in the best spirit but without cheating. I do not think there is anything more harmful to others and to ourselves than deceit.

This is the most important for me, deceit and specially self-deceit. Because to deceive the other first we have to deceive ourselves, believing that this is the way out or the best option. The grave thing is how many times we are aware of our lies, from the more serious ones to the more simple ones. We take lies as a simple mechanism that 'makes life lighter and easy'. We do not see the gravity in what it means to lie to solve something, to get out of a problem. We lie because we feel lazy to explain others why we do things this or the other way. To not explain, it is easier to lie and tell each person what they want to hear. Deep inside we know it is so but on the surface we reject it. When someone questions our honesty, the mental pattern of 'I always tell the truth' gets immediately activated. If we take this seriously and we see the couple relationship as a great opportunity to be honest, after some time of enjoying the benefits we can dare to be honest with one, with two, with a thousand, with all relationships.

Religion and politics

In the social field, religion and politics are relative equals to the mind-heart duality. When the first man in a far away tribe lifted the heaviest club and put order according to his understanding, he created the first seat of office or public representative, the first politician. Probably at the moment when the first man or woman achieved that unique feeling of love and gratefulness observing that fire that warmed their rustic life, the first priest or priestess emerged. As they say, the rest is history...

The truth is that at the dawn of humanity, human groups identified their religious and political leaders clearly and early. The prosperity of their societies depended greatly on the relationship between these characters. This is a very clear fractal representation of the same relationship reason-feeling that happens in every human being. When the 'reason' of a people listens to and respects its own feeling, these people progress. On the contrary, when the active, 'reasonable' part ignores, subdues or usurps the counterpart, this people could achieve great expansion but never true wisdom and progress. When political power subdues religious power through weapons, strength or coercion: society losses balance, direction. It is a very fragile and precarious relationship because both powers utilize their methods to achieve their goals. Political-military power does not hesitate to use violence to achieve its goals whereas violence will never be the path for the truly religious, nor even to defend their legitimate rights.

What happens when politicians in their immeasurable greed for power invade and infiltrate the religious space and do not go short in ways to achieve their goals? What we are watching nowadays: a completely unbalanced society. A good society model is reached when political power regulates, modulates and respects religious power and the latter inspires, support and limits the former. A good political leader is not a synonym for a military dictator. Quite the contrary, it is a statesperson conscious of the present and future needs of his society who has great organizational talent and a special gift to reach agreements for the common good. A good religious leader is that sensitive and imaginative human being that is able to adequate and express the greatest universal truths in the clearest way possible so that even the man and woman with the simplest understanding can comprehend and love those truths.

Theology and myths

The amazing stories of all religions in the world that translate cosmic universal truths into myths and legends. How and when do they loose their symbolic magic and become declared dogmas? When do they loose their wonderful charm and become perverse, threatening instruments capable to condemn everyone that doubt them? Dogmas, weather of faith or however they call them only serve for me to recognize the obscure hand of bad politicians disguised as priests. If we look again at the characteristics of our reason-feeling duality and we remember that in essence feeling unites and reason separates, religions are a clear product of the mind and not of the heart.

It is also good to know that in every person there is potentially a political and a religious leader and many times due to laziness or indifference we have yielded and lost the political spaces. It is not only about pointing at the negative and feeling like victims, we also have to learn to sanely defend our political and religious spaces, each one in their society.

The axis of existence and the axis of love

Our sacred symbol, our sacred cross that divides manifestation and the universe in four territories is composed of two axes that cross each other in the middle. I relate the horizontal one with existence and the vertical one with love.

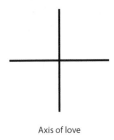

Axis of love

Many people refuse to recognize any type of hierarchical structure we are part of whether we want to or not. This conflict with 'authority' is typical of an infant state of mind.

The most sensitive or intuitive minds do not find any conflict in accepting that there will always be a brother one step higher willing to help us and another one step bellow giving us the opportunity to serve them. To be able to accept the actual level we are at, it is necessary to renounce the habit of measuring and comparing ourselves with others. Each one is the way they are and they occupy a place in the human family, if you are temporary and relatively higher, it is to help and serve those that are lower. If the consciousness of your position in life is real, you will see that there is no space for boasting or arrogance, all is occupied with the consciousness of responsibility.

When we are not yet conscious that our initial awakening starts with realizing the existence of these two original principles —existence and love, positive and negative, masculine and feminine—, it is like we lived in a world of one dimension, horizontal. Everything is flat, we are all equal, there is nobody different, we simply exist, there is no superior or inferior. This is true but it is just one part of the truth. When our understanding of duality grows, it automatically generates the sense of the vertical —love— and we recognize that this initial horizontal dimension is not the only one that exists, so does the vertical plane and we start seeing things in another way. Of course we are equal in one sense. Each drop of your blood is as precious as mine or anyone else's. But in another sense, in the vertical plane we all occupy different places in the axis of love and the real proof of how high we have elevated in the axis of love is in our respect to all beings no matter where they are at.

On one hand this rejection to authority is comprehensible, especially in times of many supposedly 'enlightened' gurus that keep taking advantage of many good willed people. Sometimes we take a while to confirm fraud and accept the pain of feeling deceived, mocked and even swindled. Many people dedicate many years of their life not only serving impostors but also making large donations to them. And the more time spent serving these fake masters, the harder and more difficult it will be to recognize and end these relationships. But this should not mine our faith or our capacity to trust that there will always be one hand above and one bellow.

Fake masters are but a good test for every pilgrim. They are the best way to test our love for truth. Only in the measure we tolerate lies and self-deceit in ourselves, these characters are able to trick us and confuse us. They build a fake and flattering relationship, they make us feel 'special', 'chosen', they give us sacred titles and trinkets they 'turn' into sacred objects and we feel grateful and we take on an almost infinite debt. All this ends when our mind gets tired of this game and decides to not accept any more lies or this type of relationship. There is no master that will help us more than ourselves. If we learn to love the truth above everything else, we will keep lies and liars away from us. Another way of approaching hierarchy is to analyze how we behave with others, always remembering that every position is relative and transitory. That is to say, one day we are above and another day we are bellow. Lets look at whom we judge and whom we understand. Judging someone places us immediately bellow in the axis of love; understanding them places us above. Lets look at it graphically: circle A holds circle B. The larger holds the smaller. The smaller will never hold the larger, except for the small part they share.

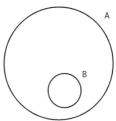

Mental patterns

¿How are they formed, how do they work and how do they dominate us later? A great part of the opinions about the mind are divided in two positions: if the mind itself is the problem or if it is good as it is. My answer is: if course it is bad itself, but it is good that it is like that because that is how it is. Simultaneity would considerably help in all fields of life because answers in many cases are 'yes and no'. There are people who believe the mind is sick by nature and the only remedy is to get rid of it. I do not exactly see it like that. This part of our being has its own process and its own developing rhythm. Same as when in babies the first part that forms is the spine which will be the base for the brain and later, the heart. That is how the different parts of our being are formed, including the mind.

When the *hardware* is practically finished the sensations start, i.e. the 'system' is tested and activity starts in the unconscious. *Hardware* connections and adjustments continue to happen even after birth. They say that in the first month we see black and white with the image inverted since the neuronal connections that allow adult vision are not created yet. In the moment we leave the maternal womb, sensations increase from 1 to 100. We pass from a state of protection where all sensations are filtered by our mother to a world of very intense, abundant and even aggressive stimuli.

A mental pattern forms as a consequence of the continuous reiteration of a thought. It is a 'way' of thinking that has been repeated countless times, produced by mechanical thinking. Each time you choose to circulate through this mental path that connects two parts of your brain through your neurons, this path strengthens and deepens like a groove. Each time it is used, it becomes deeper and easier to access. Mental patterns are like rivers through which more and more water is flowing carving its riverbed deeper. So much that before you realize, it has become a great canyon practically voiding the possibility to change the course of your thoughts or emotions. After a few years of life in this way, we have these wide rivers through which our thoughts flow and it takes an immense amount of effort to change them.

Mental patterns are part of the mechanical function of the mind and they help us to not have to think everything a thousand times, but we cannot build our lives and even less dream about transforming ourselves supported only by this part of the mind. Taking into account that our story actually starts months before birth, I take this opportunity to make a very brief but important commentary about the typical births in western hospital system encouraged mostly by this culture of fear.

Our eyes have never seen the light. However, from the first moment we get blinded by the horrible lighting in the operating room they hang us upside down and if we do not scream they hit us. First message you learn: you have to scream to not get hit. After this abuse you look for your mother's protection, that body that held you and that you love like your own. But no, the torture is not over, they cut the cord, they separate you from your mother, your protector and a lady that looks at you with a mixture of disgust and tenderness because you are all 'dirty' covered in blood takes you to take a bath. That is how our entrance to society starts. They wash us, dry us and put shampoo and perfume full of chemicals that everyone knows are carcinogenic but no one cares. This happens in the best of cases, in 'natural' births, which are the minority. The majority are C-sections, they claim it is to avoid risks but we all know that it is more comfortable and profitable for doctors.

Wouldn't you believe that with this welcoming to the world, this little mind has the right to become sick? The answer is absolutely not. Lets look at an exactly opposite case: a child is born at home through a natural birth, no problems, it doesn't cry so no need to hit him, he simply breathes, they place him in his mother's arms without cutting the cord, he knows immediately what he has to do, he sucks and feels the sweetness of the first drops of that amazing liquid that will guarantee his existence. Which of these two children do you think will have the healthiest mind? There is no way of knowing. Anyone could think that the natural born child would definitely have a healthier mental shape, but it is not necessarily so. Please know I am not saying it does not matter how our children are born, quite the contrary. Of course it is very important. Every single detail of what a true natural birth really is has to be taken into account and avoid all aggressions that newborns endure. What I am trying to say is that even if we do everything possible to save the child from unnecessary trauma and pain, this does not guarantee that these children will have a 'healthy' mind.

Lets continue our story. Either of the children, the one born in the love of his home and the one mistreated in the hospital will have the same opportunities to heal or not heal their own mind. To better understand the example we must see this through the *quadripartition* system. Lets imagine it is not two but four children, two born at home and two in the hospital. The first one born at home will thank his parents all his life for the care they had with the birth. The second one born at home will blame his parents all his life for feeling 'different', for being raised different than the rest of the kids. With the best intentions, parents probably never bought him sweets, junk food, video games or television. The first child born in a hospital will be a doctor and conscious of the suffering he experienced at birth, he will work hard to change and humanize the hospital birth system. The second one born in the hospital will be depressed, ungrateful and will never forgive his parents or life for the 'injustices' he suffered. What determines the response in these four different cases? On the one hand, the information one brings —obviously inherited from our parents— and on the other hand, the mental patterns each one has built throughout their life.

You complain about life? Do you want me to tell you about mine to see if my tragedy is greater than yours so you feel better? I can tell you the same story in the shape of a comedy or a tragedy but this is not important. The important thing is to realize that everything that happened, happens and will happen to us is 'pure medicine'. This is what some call 'the magic of changing the past'. The impossibility of getting out of the absurd drama state we live in is due to our present situation and our mental patterns, not to our past. Even for the most foolish, present unhappiness comes from the future. They could have had a good past and present, but they live terrified of the future. What will happen tomorrow? What if something bad happens to me?

Lies and apocalyptic prophecies are the daily bread for the sects dedicated to spread intrigue and fear. The story tells that when year 1000 was coming close many people committed suicide thinking the world was coming to an end. Later they postponed the date 1000 years and nowadays, modern opportunists hold on to new dates. Next one is 2012. The noble Mayan Calendar has been turned into a horoscope. The market is always grabbing the sacred to turn it into a *souvenir*. The world situation is so precarious that I would not be surprised if we don't make it to 2012. I also would not be surprised if the agony of this old order lasted a few more decades.

The lifestyle of modern humans is the perfect justification for this consumerist and highly irresponsible economic model. Those who believed the market would resolve all their problems were truly naïve or malicious. The market will never be conscious of the true human necessities. We have placed our lives in the hands of a psychopath called market., When the first warnings about global warming were made two decades ago, taunts from official experts did not wait; 'it is just a bunch of 'green' radicals, ex communists that want to cause panic' they said. Now that we are suffering the first consequences of global warming, their discourse is: 'it is already too late, there is nothing we can do'. We would have to schedule at least a 20-year world recession and face the social and political consequences this would generate, and in this way observe the extent of the irreparable damage our elegant way of life has caused. In spite of everything, it is worth trying to change now instead of sitting down to wait for some *tsunami*, glaciations or earthquakes to destroy us. You need to radically change your way of life and consume less and less all the unnecessary things the system sells as indispensable. You have to find a connection that exists between a life more and more artificial and global warming. Inform yourself, I beg you.

I am not looking for guilty ones in the past, present of future. Guilt does not exist, it is just one of the major diseases of our mind. We also cannot accuse our circumstances. Many people think they define the being, I do not see it this way. The capacity of response of human beings is amazing and unpredictable and any situation or circumstance can be the best or the worst that happens to them. Now the big question is: what does our answer depend on in the face of circumstances? It depends only and exclusively on our mind, on the *software* we are using, on our mental patterns.

Lets go back to our newborn. Since he came to the world he starts to experiment more and more visual, auditory, tactile, smell and other sensations. He is registering all these experiences and creating reactions according to instinct. With an excess of light he closes the eyes; with a door banging he gets startled, when a stranger approaches, he rejects them. That is to say, he is forming the initial pattern that is the duality of acceptance-rejection. The child learns that there are things he likes and things he does not like. The pattern of differentiation is created at the same time. At the beginning the child lives in unity, there is nothing in him that tells him he is separate from the world and other things. Him and his breast are one, he does not even think about it but gradually the perception arises that sometimes there is breast and sometimes there is not because suddenly he is hungry and there is not breast. At that instant he cries to express discomfort. From that point on he becomes more conscious every day that the breast and him are different.

In some part of his mind he knows that 'him' and his 'breast' exist, the me and the not-me.

Then he starts to recognize more elements. He discovers that beyond that huge omnipresent breast there is another huge body that he loves infinitely. Later he continues to identify other objects, rattle, blanket, dolls —not-mes—. This is the origin of ego, the pattern of differentiation. From this point on this little being will have thousands of experiences that he will manage with his acceptance-rejection pattern, leaving the purely intuitive aside in order to incorporate the information of his genetic code. That is to say, the acceptance-rejection patterns of his parents: more sugar, less sugar, I don't like pumpkin, I love apples.

We keep advancing, we are a year and a half old and we have learned to walk, we know what falling is and we know pain. At the same time we also recognize pleasure, we are starting to perceive the great duality. What are our first thoughts, our first analysis of a situation? We like pleasure; pain makes us cry so we seek to endlessly repeat everything that gives us pleasure. 'I always want to eat apple pie, I don't want to fall or eat pumpkin'. We have the third pattern there, polarization: always pleasure, never pain.

By the time my daughter was almost two years old, we had made an effort for some time to not say the word 'mine' in front of her. We knew that word did not exist in some American languages so every time we played with her it was always *our* doll, *our* ball and so on. But one day at lunch one of her brothers suddenly grabbed her spoon and with the fierceness of a two-year-old girl she yelled 'mine!'. My wife and I looked at each other abashed by this reality. We later discovered that a boy she played with had transmitted to her the most powerful western secret: 'mine' —fourth pattern—. However, even if she had not had any contact with someone that communicated that word to her, the thought of possession already was in her DNA through our inheritance and, sooner or later she would have expressed it.

With this fourth pattern we have the columns to build all our personality. From this point we could detail a long list of new patterns but it is good to let you recognize both common patterns and your own. There is a mental pattern behind each emotion. Try to see how they activate, how they function and how they condition us, hidden in emotions like anger, envy, happiness, jealousy, bragging, humility and even tenderness.

We have two or three years accepting and rejecting, differentiating the world from us and differentiating us from the world, we are convinced that we only want to live in pleasure; we have learned that sometimes lying helps us to prolong enjoyment and our patrimony grows. We have more toys, more clothes and more belongings. We learn to differentiate and value people by what the gift us. The majority of vices are formed, distortion is ready. I do not know what naïve person said that children are pure. I am sure they never had sons, daughters or nephews. I am also not saying they are pure selfishness but there are certain parts of the mind that are formed wrongly and almost mechanically. And we have to take them from error to clarity at the right moment. Generally speaking, we will have to correct the majority of the mental patterns built until age 17 or 18.

I am sure the universe does not care if I do not agree with the formative stages of the mind the way life created them. Why is our mind like it is? I do not know. It could be a thousand different ways and rest assured we would still not agree. What I do know is the mind is as it is, if you look at it well, if you observe it well, one day you will be able to change it and reeducate it.

The limits of the mind

One of the most important and difficult necessities we have is to observe the limits of our mind. It is one of the practices that must be present in your attempt of transformation form the beginning. The first step is simply to watch and observe. This is very important in order for you to really see and not imagine what you see. To see the limit of your mind does not mean you will immediately transcend it. This is achieved with an act of extreme sincerity. It is a practice that has many benefits because not only you get to know yourself deeply —to the limit— but you put to work the not so used muscle of honesty. Many times when people come and tell me about the books they read and their spiritual practices, the image comes of the donkey with the carrot tied up on a stick in front of its nose. Even if the donkey walks eternally he will never achieve the goal: to eat the carrot.

You can see the limit of your mind every time something collides heads first with your system of beliefs. Every time something attacks, questions or contradicts them you hear a voice inside that screams: 'nooooo'. This denial is precisely marking the limit of your mind. What follows is simple. We can take two directions here. The first one would be to enter and absurd conversation whether you are crazy for questioning all beliefs to measure the limit of your mind; and the second one is to simply see the limit of your mind. Did you see it?

With the example of the donkey I tried to provoke a rejection reaction to facilitate you to identify your limits. This is only the first step, you don't need to change anything, just observe and practice every time something touches the limit of your mind, just be attentive. Once you know your limit in all areas of your life, moving the boundaries to positions ever more flexible will be a matter of little time. On the contrary, if the milestones of your beliefs are of reinforced concrete, I apologize. At least I do not think there is anything I can do.

The teachings

When people take teachings from books or 'masters' that merely repeat how things were 1000 or 100 years ago without any adaptation to present circumstances, people get even more confused. I do not deny their good intentions but they are not enough. They naively do all kinds of strange practices with objectives beyond their immediate realization in the best of cases. They dream with levitating or telepathy but are incapable to stop lying or deceiving themselves.

What gives value to a teaching is its aliveness. The teaching comes directly from the fountain of life through someone that is connected to that fountain. The truth never changes in essence but it needs constant adaptation in its form. At each time and in every second the truth ought to be reinterpreted, rethought according to the mind of each being we want to address. While the teaching will be a certain way for someone, it will be a very different way for another. We cannot freeze the truth or the teaching because in less time than what it takes to think about it, they slip from us and they already need another change. Truth will always be an eternal fugitive due to its simultaneous double nature. It is there and it is not there, it always is and it is not, like light: wave and particle, simple and complex, absolute and relative, volatile and eternal. Besides, total truth will always be beyond and above our perceptions.

Once the channel stops working and disappears, the hundreds of books left about that teaching are mostly senseless because what you read out of context can confuse more than clarify. We have seen this after the death of the great masters of the last century. The abyss between the master and the next generation is exaggerated. The teaching starts to get distorted; it collapses and ends up becoming a contradiction.

A teaching can be given to a person in an apparently opposite way it is given to another person. What is medicine for one is poison for another. During thousands of years people were only preoccupied with planting more wheat to calm the stomach and accumulate material things and they had to be urged to occupy themselves with spiritual things. Nowadays we must see it complementary. Enough of thinking only about spirit, let us honor our matter and help to stop the destruction of mother earth.

Photographs instead of movies

The greatest obstacle to change our mind is that the mind will be the first to get the information and it simply does not agree with any substantial change. It will criticize and try to discredit —with any possible argument— any information that threatens the stability of the patterns it created with which it 'dominates' every situation.

Imagine that the doorman of a company gets fired with a letter from the main branch. He will obviously be the one that receives the letter. Do you think he will give it to his immediate boss? That is how our mind works. While you read your mind will not stop questioning this proposal from its own trench but there are many things that filter through and in the end it is not just about paper and letters but mostly energy directed to your heart, to your intuition.

This mental pattern of defense is very awkward and is worth dedicating a few lines to. We find ourselves again in front of the great question: what is truly your being? Who are you? Like I said from the beginning I much rather you answer someday but what I can tell you is that your mind is just a part of you, it is not you. Your job is to observe who uses whom so you can free yourself from all confusion; that is to say, if you utilize your mind or if it utilizes you.

Our mind is a mechanism of sorts that creates its own mechanisms. It creates automatic procedures based on accumulated information to not have to think about the same thing millions of times. Once we learn to walk we don't have to think how to walk. This is an amazing function. But problems arise when you try to apply this mechanical function to human relationships or simply to all events you have to face without discriminating which system of thought to use and due to habit or laziness you let the mechanical system operate. I would say that one of our greatest problems is laziness. We have to learn to live in the tireless attempt to use the mechanical part only when strictly necessary.

Life is like a movie where everything is in constant movement and our mind likes to take photos and freeze images of situations and people and put them in a file. From there it issues judgments, it establishes behavior patterns and it even predicts how people will behave in different situations. It loves statistics and generalizations. The mind says: 'Juan is like this and Pedro always behaves in this way'. It does not take into account that Juan and Pedro are human beings that change and evolve.

There are things in life that are definitely mechanical but there are many that are not and the mind feels sort of insecure and intimidated by the latter. The mind wants to control everything, predict, anticipate and feel secure. It is by definition contrary to the nature of life. The paradox is that even though it is coiling, changing and unstable the mind does not tolerate changes and even less without its permission. It does not like to loose control because it takes it some time to adapt. And the most contradictory feature is that it despises monotony and it is always eager for new sensations.

Level of fragmented consciousness and mind

One of the greatest mistakes our mind makes it to believe we have a stable level of consciousness. Our consciousness flows like a wave in time. Sometimes it is up and sometimes down.

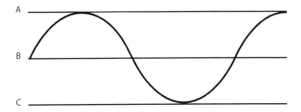

Line A represents the highest level of consciousness, line B is the middle level and line C is unconsciousness. At some point of the day, week or month we all have consciousness at its highest level and we then understand the most elevated things and we make the deepest reflections. But what happens? Time goes by and this state dissolves, it is gradually lost, circumstances change, we stop reading that 'spirituality' book or we finish an 'elevated' conversation with a friend or with some master and we have to carry on with life and solve countless trivialities: work, shop, fixing the car. We go from being transcendental beings to simple people absorbed in everyday chores. Maybe four hours go by and we don't feel altruist love emotions so intensely, we become cold and calculating to be able to solve practical things. Our level of consciousness has changed but we have not noticed.

We only have the remembrance of fragments of consciousness but the connecting thread that links them does not exist. Then by accident someone attacks us, offends us, steps on our foot and doesn't even apologize. Furthermore they blame us and we get enraged, we yell at them, insult them not only for their carelessness but for their unconsciousness, for their lack of respect, for causing us pain, for stepping on our foot and without even apologizing properly. At this moment the worst thing that can happen to us is a person close to us saying: 'drop it, don't be angry'. There is nothing more enraging in the world than somebody telling us not to be enraged when we are enraged. It is like putting out a fire with gasoline. We immediately get enraged with our friend because 'he doesn't understand us' and we give them all possible arguments to

CHAPTER II | THE GREAT DUALITY

justify our rage. Our mental pattern of 'spirituality' does not admit our rage, justified or not, so we don't accept neither that we are enraged nor that it was an accident to run into such a foolish person.

We are not capable of seeing and accepting that our level of consciousness is at its lowest expression. We have to let rage pass, cool down and slowly recuperate our 'average' level. But what happens if at the most intense moment of our anger we accept our rage and recognize there are emotions that overflow us, that we are not perfect, that life is full of nasty accidents and that we have to be tolerant, sometimes exaggeratedly flexible and recover our good mood as soon as possible because for the most part our rage will only hurt us? Therefore, the quickest we can recognize our mood the faster we can redirect our line of consciousness to ascend.

Our mental patterns block our consciousness. Because of this we are not able to see when we lie or when we are enraged. Because there is a very powerful mental pattern that hides these negative things 'we don't do'. It tells us: 'we don't behave that way'. At that moment, consciousness is interrupted and it jumps from one segment to another. It is like editing a movie, we cut out the part we don't like. When we develop the 'witness', the observer, we accompany and it is consciousness throughout all its levels and we do not doubt to dive temporarily into all the negative emotions because the important thing at that stage is not to have them or not, but to be conscious of them.

The illusion of I

When we consider our internal reality, there is not greatest damage or futile illusion than to believe in a consolidated I. This mental pattern of always believing we are better than what we are gets nullified if we can remember the harsh reality: we do not even have an I. There are normally a series of characters within us, individuals forming, each one with their own interests, their own dreams, and their own contradictions. It is not as simple as saying there is a good and bad part. No! It is much more complex. Within us —in our mind— not only live a people or a nation, but many nations. It is very important to observe that there is not one I but many.

We are used to lie to obtain what we want and we apply this same pattern both to our exterior and to our interior processes. These inner characters are usually fighting for supremacy and they do not doubt to use lies or boycott to prevail. This is one of the main causes of our self-deceit.

A character inside you wants to love the truth but there are 50 others that do not want it, do not look for it, they are not interested in it. Someone within is concerned to have a good relationship with mother earth but the other 50 do not want to loose even a pinch of their comfort to contaminate a bit less. This little ecologic I has 50 voices against him that will try to lie —distort reality— bringing up all kinds of 'rational' arguments, even scientific ones to prevent the conscious character to win terrain.

This is how societies, institutions and families function. They are formed by individuals with no real I, they are not 'units'. It is illusory to ask them for a commitment or a word because the one signing the contract is not the one that will go to work. To get out of the entanglements our characters create for our life, we invent a thousand excuses as to why we act a certain way. We frequently make a fool of ourselves pretending to deceive others because many people realize we say something and we do the opposite.

We lie to save our public image —which is truly what we love the most— in order to hide the sea of contradictions within and in this way avoid our fables and our chaos to be discovered. We have to mount a better story every time, a biggest lie, even a philosophy or a religion that justify us. We love to impersonate the character of a coherent person. We spend life justifying ourselves in front of others just to improve our social image. But of all these characters: who is in control? How does the consecutive rotation happen among our fragments in taking the control of our life?

I think there are three aspects than influence this. The first is there are characters that are stronger or more dominant, more frequent and more developed. The second one is that with the minimal consciousness we have —1% or 2% of our potential— we can surround ourselves with influences that resonate with the character we want to reinforce. That is how we choose food, music, reading, clothing, friendships, and activities. All that influences the characters. In third place, we must consider the fortuitous nature of life itself that in some moments becomes decisive.

When I speak of a fragmented mind I am not only referring to the absence of memory or connection among different moments of our mind, but also to the succession in the control of our life each character has, which all curiously call themselves I. Imagine you call a house occupied by 50 people but only one phone. They all are called Pedro and most of them are myth maniacs. Who do you leave a message for?

The art is to fix your internal 'country', to first recognize all its characters and pacify them, then initiate a dialog among all of them until wars and internal sabotages are over, and lastly to choose a life project that can move forward. We definitely cannot carry on all our interests, especially if they are contradictory. Many will have to be left behind. This is one of the things we have to be very clear about so as not to drag thoughts for life like 'I should have done this or that'. What is important is that all decisions have to be taken from a deep place and not from the surface of our mind driven by our mental patterns and dragged by blind and mechanical forces that in the end will only bring us pain. Decisions like who to raise a family with or what profession to follow deserve the preparation of a sacred space-time which allow us to choose from the utmost depth. Spaces like the Vision Quest or similar rituals take greatest importance in times of so much confusion.

Do you really know what you want?

One of the most difficult things to achieve in life is to know what you really want at this moment of your evolution. What do you want in the first, second and third place? Until you are not clear about this, your progress will be a big challenge because both your energy and your efforts will be divided. You must be absolutely honest with yourself. If you still want to entertain yourself for a while, do not say you want to walk a sacred path. If you still want to play with sex and accumulate beautiful experiences, do not say you want to form a family. The majority of things are not good or bad in themselves but in their context. The relativity of things is another sense of the quadripartition. There exist a relative good and a relative bad, an absolute good and an absolute bad. For me the absolute good is honesty and the absolute bad is lie. The main problem is not to have three lovers at the same time, but lying to keep them.

The greatest teaching I received on my fourth Vision Quest after fasting for thirteen days is that life expresses through us in four ways and these are our four doors: what you feel, what you think, what you say and what you do. When you get what you feel, what you think, what you say and what you do to be in the same line, your path straightens. Generally we feel something, we think something else, we say the contrary and we do whatever else. For this reason it is necessary to know what you want in order to achieve your goals, to not repress anything, to not postpone your true desires. Is it sex you want? Then have it in a fair and transparent way, do not deceive anybody. You want money? Earn it in the most dignified way possible. You want power? Make and effort to deserve trust. When you have achieved everything in a fair way you will be able to leave it with no pain, with no complaint. The trap is in how much sex, money and power you want for yourself before transcending them.

It is something very simple, elemental. Someone that takes what doesn't belong to them does not know the pleasure of honesty. Someone that enjoys cheating on his or her partner does not yet discover the pleasure of honesty. Loyalty and honesty are not a moral issue. I see them in relation to our level of mental development. What do you truly enjoy?

The mind starts learning, refining itself and at the beginning it enjoys very basic things but as it evolves it discovers new forms of true pleasure, each time less conditioned by selfishness. In the end morals is just a mechanism of social containment, an instrument of repression, another conditioning factor, nothing else. It is about learning to do things because they are good and because we enjoy doing good. It is evident that morals are necessary for certain groups because they have to be told it is not good to kill, steal, lie etc. But what has to be developed is the pleasure to do good, to speak good, to think good. Repression does not bring lasting results. Repressing is like pushing on springs. As soon as you get tired or distracted, they go back to their original shape. One cannot change oneself through repression. My proposal is to change through pleasure. Through love. One stops lying when he or she loves and enjoys a truth more than a lie, one stops smoking when one loves pure air more than nicotine in the lungs. If you truly love your partner, your family, your children, love will make you at least think twice before bringing more suffering to those you say you love. The question is: how much do you really want what you say you want? This is the heart of the matter.

We commit to a relationship, we form a family, we have children when we still do not know ourselves enough and we are not yet conscious of our incoherencies. We believe we love our partner but after a few years we do nothing but attack and underestimate each other because the relationship became and obstacle to our other interests. All human beings are very similar in this, we have many interests, usually contradictory but our fragmented mind does not perceive it in this way. It jumps from one subject to another and creates conflicts without caring much about the damage it is causing. They do not teach us to be sincere placing all our interests on the table, nor they teach us to moderately solve our contradictions and priorities.

Memory

Another important subject is memory, remembrance. I am not talking about the memory of the mind, the one capable to remember 50 phone numbers, names, addresses, birthdays. I am talking about the memory of the observer, the memory of consciousness, of the witness. Test it in the following way: for 15 minutes try to be attentive in a totally uninterrupted way to the sensation produced by the air in the tip of your nose every time it goes in and out. If you get distracted, start over again. This simple exercise can clearly show you the functioning of your mind with relation to time and consciousness.

Our fragmented mind jumps from one thought to the next and does not remember with the same intensity or clarity what it thought or said just moments ago. The memory we are talking about is the flowing of consciousness with relation to time, our fourth dimension. We come back to our great duality, our great space-time binary. It is not just about being conscious of what happens in a space with its dimensions —long, tall and deep— but also of how much time we are capable to 'sustain' this consciousness uninterruptedly. How long is the intermission between one conscious moment and the next?

Misunderstandings or wrong teachings about time are very frequent. They want to deny its reality or underestimate it in the same way they tried to do with matter. Time is as sacred a reality as Space, it is a primordial energy and it exists from the start of creation itself. For me it is my father just as Space is my mother. The confusion is in our stereotypical and primitive way of measuring it. Again, our dual logic clashes with the possibility of a relative time and it only accepts a mechanical time. And the truth is there are many 'times' and they all coexist.

Remember how long days or hours become when a great effort is being done or when going through a painful trial and how they fly when we are enjoying ourselves. Our perception of time varies according to our emotions. Because of this, if any of the spiritual achievements you think you have has not passed the test of time —the fourth door— do not consider it real.

We cannot say we understand quaternary or quadripartition until we have traversed countless times this sequence of one, two, three, four and remember it…Take into account that trying to understand or explain this is just that, and approximation, an attempt from some point in this infinite spiral.

The ego

It is not a sinister representative placed inside us as a divine punishment. It can be like the cocoon that wraps us and protects us while we grow and mature and that in due time we have to let go of.

The ego is our offering, what we raise from childhood and we feed and decorate. It is the sheep we raise and fatten for the town party. Since it is very small, we know we are going to offer it but we do not give it less love for that reason. In the world there are people in very different levels of evolution. Whereas for some it is time to present their offering, for others it is time to fatten it. What are we doing bringing a skinny sheep to the party?

Many need an opportunity to grow, realize themselves, be happy, study, work, have a family and give them a dignified life. They do not need a religion to tell them: 'suffer brother because suffering purifies'. How useful is it to tell a depressed, crushed by the system 'third world' man 'brother renounce to the material, get interested in the spiritual'? How useful is it to renounce an ego he does not have because his self-esteem is on the floor? The secret is in knowing when to 'kill the little pig'.

Judeo-Christian culture

I would like that this work of transformation did not imply such painful inner changes sometimes, but this is honestly not possible and it is good to know now. Changes are not themselves painful but what hurts us is to let go of many beliefs that are exactly what is hindering our advance.

The real problem is that we are totally identified with our mind, with our beliefs and at the bare sign of a critique or question about them; we jump like we were pierced with a spear or like they touched our most sacred thing. Calm. The first thing to learn is that beliefs are just that and they are in the mind. They are *part* of your being; they are not your being. They are not and will never be the most sacred thing there is in you. Of course they are respectable in their own universe. There can be some more or less wrong or more or less accurate, but they will always be beliefs. Any thoughtful person will remember how many times in life they changed their ideology and could become enemies with people or with the world for this reason. In any case, the attachment to our beliefs is the proof of what grade of fundamentalism one is at.

We all know religious wars exist and that systems like the inquisition existed for the extermination of different ideas. Even though the inquisition systems have ended, the effects of this science of torment have not disappeared. We must be extremely just and prudent when we examine ancient teachings and paradigms that run and define our interior world. We are seriously affecting the planet with our ideologies. Some teaching may have already fulfilled certain purposes in our evolution —which can always be discussed together with their intentions— but even wanting to believe the motivation was good, I find necessary to clarify some things and reject others for considering them highly harmful.

I coincide with many people that study different cultures and propose alternatives to this devouring and hegemonic system we call western culture, in which beyond its enrichment and maturity thanks to many other contradictions, its true roots are found in what we call Judeo-Christianism. Thus it is much more appropriate to use the term 'Judeo-Christian culture' than 'western culture'. Besides, the latter alludes to a geographical differentiation that is little real, particularly taking into account that within this geographic territory —the west— cultures have existed and still exist with a diametrically opposed conception of life.

It is necessary to make and important clarification at this point. I recognize Jesus of Nazareth as one of the great masters of humanity and his teachings as a very important contribution. However, not all who call themselves Christian honor the wisdom of the great master. Quite the contrary, imitating a modern franchise, they seized the 'brand name' ignoring the deep sense of his message: love. I cannot avoid to point out how century after century they gradually turned noble teachings into a completely opposite practice. Like throwing a rock in the center of a pond; the expansion circles that move away from the center change their polarity to the point of expressing the opposite energy. This is a law for all cases.

In this century, far from adopting a universal understanding of the equality and sacredness of all traditions, the majority of Christian churches seem to act as political movements more preoccupied with proselytism than with religious work. Particularly in South America, this grave attack against what is left of our cultures and sacred traditions continues. The argument still remains of 'the true religion' and 'the word of god' with which they keep invading and destroying our traditions. Today it is not only imperative to ask for forgiveness but to make a public statement recognizing the validity and dignity of all native religions in the world. This would not relieve much the damage and pain caused throughout centuries but it would help a lot those that still today agree with and believe the crimes committed in the name of 'faith' are necessary. In these times silence can be the biggest accomplice.

In a few centuries, the noble members, saints and martyrs became part of a powerful political machinery with the mission to destroy and wipe from the face of the earth every conception or culture that does not accept their holy dogmas. They went from being hunted to being hunters, from being martyrs to martyring others, destroying a long list of peoples and cultures on their path, starting with European traditions like the Celtics, Basques, Bretons, Gallics, Vikings and many more. They imposed with blood and sword held by the power on duty. And this new Judeo-Christian culture brought as message salvation through love… Like Ricardo Espinosa would say: 'God is love, lets kill anyone that disagrees'.

The ability of politicians to confuse us has been remarkable throughout the history of humanity. It is astonishing that by manipulating a discourse, a teaching that is true in essence, it is possible to materialize the opposite. I am not judging religious leaders. I am pointing out the ability of political leaders to infiltrate religious movements and even direct them.

After consolidating power and hegemony in Europe, guided by true blind faith, the Judeo-Christian culture moves to other lands carrying 'the word of god' and the evangelic message, 'bringing the true faith', 'destroying the darkness and ignorance of the pagan world'. Without doubt they almost succeeded. Had not life and the universe had other plans, they would have 'extirpated' not just our worship. They did not know that the main cult in the universe is diversity in all its forms: cultural, religious, biologic.

They built a dogmatic culture in which questioning their divine revelation carried a death penalty. With terror, they created unquestionable 'truths' that after 2000 years of fear and psychological and physical torture have succeeded in that the majority of their believers do not question much. Very normal and healthy things like analyzing, debating and even doubting were turned into synonyms of blasphemy and heresy. All things that are never doubted, never questioned, never aired end up stinking. The great majority of people never even dared to wonder if the words written in the 'sacred books' of all the religions in the world, as beautiful and wise as the seem, have been really written by God or if they were rather the inspiration of a 'good man'. Quotation marks are there because I do not believe someone that lies about the authorship of his writings is so good.

I do not believe God has written absolutely anything. His/her creation, the universe speaks for itself and in every language for whoever wants to listen and knows how to actually 'read the book of life'. I do believe some scriptures might have been 'inspired' by forces, energies or understandings superior to the human mind but I also believe that the bulk of these 'sacred scriptures' is a human creation that, trying to gain credibility and acceptance, resorts to the signature of divinity instead of modestly taking responsibility for the authorship of the work. This is one of the darkest points in religions. I prefer to think that the act of usurping the divine signature for human creations is more the product of mystical deliriums than premeditated deceit and bad intention. I admire more a person that proposes an idea, writes it and signs it —even if times shows it was no so accurate— than one that asserts that what he wrote was the word of God and threatens with eternal damnation all those who do not believe him. The fact someone even tries to pretend to intimidate us in this way is a grave lack of respect to freedom and human dignity.

We can continue to believe it was mystical delirium and not bad intention. But that does not save us from the damage that happened, happens and that will continue to happen until we return dignity to the other traditions. This is also not about ignoring all the positive things religions have contributed to human beings. We have to give them again the opportunity to fulfill the mission of *religar*, not from the old paradigm of man with God, but to *religar* our *reason* with our *feeling*. I ask that they do not sentence us to eternal damnation for not believing that they are not the only representatives of the God of love; that they understand that as humanity it is urgent to come to great agreements among human beings.

I write these lines mostly for good those willed people that belong to religious movements and live waiting to see some progress in their consciousness in this life. Thus I want to tell you with all tenderness that nothing built on lies will bring any progress in consciousness. Maybe a good tactic would be to ignore all deception, not point it out and not talk about the negative aspects like the concrete damage some religions cause but in reality I do not pretend to follow a 'winning' strategy. My commitment is with reality and with my people that still struggle for survival against the daily destruction in the name of 'God'. I do not believe all religious atrocities are necessary or that there always have to be a perfect spiritual argument to justify them. My proposal is directed towards simple men and women that are waiting for a little signal from the universe to show them where their path to follow goes.

Some years ago, the morning after a beautiful ayahuasca ceremony I was transplanting small cauliflowers from a seedbed to their definite place. One of the participants of the ceremony came over. He was a young man from a big city in the north of the planet. His heart was as big as his smile. His eyes were shining with joy as he approached crossing the plot where I was planting. When he got next to me he asked softly: 'can I help you?' I answered him with another smile: 'sure but first please step off the cauliflowers'. He had not realized that on his way to me he had killed several dozens of freshly transplanted cauliflowers and was standing on one when he stopped walking.

It is not just about having the most pure and noble intention, a clean mind free of dogmas is also necessary, and this allows us to honestly evaluate the possible damage of our good intentions. First we have to know where we are standing. It is easy to erase 5000 years of culture for some, for others these last five centuries were just a small dark phase. Thus I want to tell all dear brothers and sisters that want to give us a hand that first we have to look very well where we are standing.

One of the greatest truths somebody ever transmitted to me is expressed simply in three words: 'everything is fine'. Something changed in me forever from the very first moment I heard this. When I shared it with friends there were some that got it immediately but there were also those that sincerely questioned it because they did not understand how in the midst of so much suffering and injustice, it was possible to pray 'everything is fine' with our people. It is certainly very difficult to understand. To pray 'everything is fine' is talking from the very heart of the creator, it means to see everything as medicine; it is total acceptance of what is happening. It means that my mind is not offering any more resistance to reality. It is to understand bad as a temporary event, but to accept everything exactly as it is. But this prayer can sometimes turn into something more dangerous than an atomic bomb because it hides the possibility of hosting error and self-negligence. When I was doing my last Vision Quest, one of the main purposes was to find reconciliation between this amazing prayer and the incomprehensible and useless suffering caused by some people that prayed in that way. After 17 days fasting in the mountain the great mystery answered: 'of course everything is fine but why can't it be better?' Even though creators made everything very well, they did not forbid us to try to improve some things, starting with ourselves.

CHAPTER III

The Ternary

The three Andean worlds

Ancient tawantinsuyans ordered their mythical and concrete space in the following way: they understood there were three worlds or three realities that interacted among them and with everything in existence.

Hanan pacha is the world on top, up high, including both the concrete and the real part —celestial bodies and stars— and the mythical (but also real) space that served as residence to many *Apus* and spirits like *Tayta Inti* —the sun—, *Mama Killa* —the moon—, *Illapa* —lightning—, *K'uychi* —the rainbow—, planets like *Qoyllur* —Venus—, *Unquy* —the Pleiades— and the *Chacana* —the very Cross of the South—, all considered divine and inhabitants of the heights.

The animal that represented this space was the majestic condor that with its impressive and elegant flight is undeniably the king of heights. The *Apus* —spirits of the mountains— are characters to this day considered members of this great family of all that exists. There are also hierarchies and peculiarities among them. For example, the *Apu* Ausangate is considered the main one in all the Cusco region. Then there are several dozens of important *Apus* up to the purely local ones. Each one of them has its own personality and characteristics. The great majority of them are considered masculine energies but there are a few also considered feminine —ñustas—. *Apus* have the capacity to protect us, heal us, give us happiness and prosperity. According to the Andean vision it is essential to maintain a very good relationship with them and have them constantly present, always offering them our respect. Even before eating or consuming something it is tradition to blow what we are about to consume in the direction of the *Apus* we want to share it with.

The *Kay Pacha* is the world of here. We cannot say 'the real world' because the three worlds are equally real. However it is understood that it refers to the world where we spend the majority of time with our ordinary consciousness, sometimes very ordinary. It is a place that acts as a bridge between the world above and the world bellow; it is a world of relationship, the door to the world above and to the world bellow. Its main characteristic is parity in complementarity.

The *Uhu pacha* is the world bellow, inhabited by certain kinds of spirits of the earth and spirits of the ancestors, where the dead go, where we burry the mummies —the *mallkis*—. It is also the world of sacred plants, of the medicine and the interior world that is within each of us. The *Uhu pacha* is also the one we ask to receive all our illnesses to transform them. It is many times said that sickness can be seen as a disorder of things —that belong to a world but are in another— and placing them in order, one recovers health.

The sacred coca leave and the payments or 'despachos'

In this system of permanent equilibrium one of the most important aspects in our live culture is the understanding or the consciousness of the exchange of energies with life, that is to say what it is traditionally known as *ayni*. To ignore this can be the cause of great sickness or at least of profound dissatisfaction. No being exists in the planet that is not taking something from life and simultaneously giving something to life. The point is how much you take and how much you give in your different levels of relationship —your family, your community, your society, your planet—.

Perceiving the relation between what we give to life and what we take form it is what will bring us true happiness. On the contrary, if we adopt a selfish and stingy attitude it will not be long before we get sick and we will be unable to enjoy the amazing situation that is to feel we have a 'favorable balance'. I give more than what I take, life flows in me, I am not a parasite sucking the energy of others.

I remember very clearly when I first went to the jungle, I traveled to different Shipibo villages accompanying my dear don Benito. One afternoon in a village we heard great rejoicing. Everybody was running towards the port. Pedro —one of don Benito's nephews— had caught a huge paiche. It was a fish longer than six feet. Pedro was happily and proudly standing by it while several skilled guys cut the giant fish with machetes. Then he started to distribute it. There was not one family that did not get a piece at no cost. He walked away with a decent piece but not much bigger than the others. His true profit? The love and respect of his community. I remember his smile to this day. Pedro was the man of the community that week, he was a channel for abundance; the next week was Juan, and Francisco the next and probably Pedro again the following one because he was a good fisherman. I saw this with my own eyes when I was 18 years old and it showed me how life was in our villages.

Nowadays, if somebody catches a fish they say 'bon appetit' and they eat it themselves. The sensation of enjoying when one gives is a traditional value of our Amazonian and Andean people that has gotten lost in modern culture, where who enjoys the most is the one that takes and consumes the most. This is understandable in societies that have lost natural and sincere ways of reward like the love and respect of the community. When Pedro shared his paiche with everybody, he was not only enjoying the pride to be a good fisherman but mainly he understood that day he was lucky and he might not be so fortunate the next day, but that did not mean there wouldn't be a piece of fish for his children.

This exchange of energies does not only happen in the human sphere but with everything around us. We must be conscious of all we receive in order to thank properly because thanking is giving, it is offering, a type of *ayni* is happening. This is the reason why from ancient times arouse the tradition to 'pay', to offer and thank mainly to who supports us and provides sustenance —our Pachamama— and also our *Apus* that look after us and protect us. This 'despacho' tradition allow us to offer all our products, our work, all things we consider noble and valuable to the *Apus* and Pachamama, we call them by their names through the sacred coca leave, our *kokamama*. She is the most noble messenger and intermediary between human beings and the inhabitants of the *Hanan pacha*.

This can only be our belief for some people but it is good that you know that plants also have a spirit and the each one has different properties, not just on a physical level. The *kokamama* has the amazing attribute of transmitting and delivering messages. That is why it is essential in all our offerings. Coca leaves are widely recognized in the Andean population for their nutritious, energetic properties and as amplifiers of consciousness. The properties of a plant can transform generation after generation the psychology of a whole culture. Those of us who love and respect the ceremonial use of coca leaves recognize the tremendous power in them. Many of us who know this sacred medicine in depth identify its magical participation in numerous features of the Andean culture.

Unlike other sacred plants with much more spectacular and flashy effects, the humble and sacred coca leaf asks for more time, patience and perseverance for us to perceive its amazing medicine. It sensitizes to the point of seeing common good, transcending all selfish attitude. How much it could help to improve relationships, specially couples, because it has the capacity to help us express very deep and sensitive things with purely kind, well intentioned words leaving aside the mental pattern that makes us offend in order to speak our truth.

I present the following reflection to have just an idea of how powerful this sacred medicine is. Power is something neutral; it depends on who manages it or who directs it. Unfortunately the coca leaf has become world famous for the use of cocaine and cocaine has become famous for the incredible amounts of money moved around it. Cocaine can buy human beings, wills and even whole governments. It can cause many deaths, wars and destroy millions of homes with addiction. All this happens when a plant of power is used outside of its tradition and with negative direction. Imagine all this power turned over to a positive, constructive side. We could not only end hunger and malnutrition in our people, but in the whole world. If it wasn't for dark interests pressing for it to stay penalized and fought against, the entire world would be enjoying its benefits and Peru would feel just like Pedro, enjoying the love and respect of the world community.

Mind, soul and religion

This is a nice triad to star talking about the ternary. Mind creates the soul and the soul creates religion, but none of them has eternal life guaranteed. However, it is all they give us to get out of this labyrinth. Mind, soul and religion are our tools that help us to find the way back.

When I affirm that religion is a fruit of the mind many will jump from their chair, some offended and others skeptical and baffled. But the intention is not to offend anybody but to clarify this proposal. For me the mind is as sacred as the heart and to say that soul and religion come from the mind is no offense. I would call the soul the most noble part of my mind, or the most sensitive one. The white dot inside the black space.

To transverse the path of the mind, soul and religion is an important part of the sacred path; moreover, it is essential, we have to attain a good mind, a good soul and a good religion. But which is the end of this path? Can we continue through eternity and it takes us to a goal? Once we understand what we have to understand we cannot continue to invent more of a path, we have to unwalk what we walked, unlearn what we learned, be free again, return to the source, to the place where confusion has not yet built a nest.

Any partial truth can also be called a lie. Mind, soul and religion are just part of the total reality and they represent partiality and diversity. They are the instruments given to us to find totality. They are the seeds of the tree of transcendence, they are not immortality. Religions are born, they reproduce and they can die just like souls and minds. Our immortality is given but only potentially. It depends on achieving consciousness, *crystalinety*. There is no more time to loose. It depends on you here and now, to achieve the necessary intensity to be alert enough and the most consciousness possible to dissolve the mental patterns that prevent you from being free and transparent as a crystal.

If we relate the mind with existence and the heart with feeling, number 3 represents the relationship between heart and mind. The fruit of their love, that is to say consciousness, the *witness*, the one that has the possibility to survive. Existence disconnected from love and love with no existence through which to express would eventually end up extinguished in their own universes. The mere possibility to achieve consciousness relating our existence with our love, our Sun with our Moon, our sky with our earth, gives us permission to dream with a possible transcendence. But I do not think eternal life is an obligation for everybody.

They say that in each average ejaculation there can be 200 million sperms and only one transcends from all of them. From this fact we can extract two ideas. The first is to remind those that go through life complaining about their bad luck that they won an amazing lottery. And the second one is that nature shows us that life is a bold struggle for transcendence, not a pusillanimous plea and even less an immortality that is undeserved and given away. And even though the possibility figures —one in 200 million— are not very encouraging it does not have to be taken literally. There is not a limited quota for conscious beings.

Put in a more clear and direct way, you only have a few years —however many your life lasts— to create a stable and solid enough consciousness that allows you to cross the death threshold. If you do not achieve it, your energy will separate from your matter and each one will go back to their source.

Love, justice and injustice

On one hand these are three levels that distinguish three types of human beings. On the other hand they are the options that the universe presents to us each time life demands an answer. To live in the level of injustice means to live permanently taking advantage of others, it does not matter if legally or illegally. The injustice is to take from others what belongs to them. To live in the level of justice is to give each one what corresponds to them but also to become aware of the unjust and illegal economy system that govern us and commit ourselves to try to generate situations that promote a better redistribution. In order to achieve love we have to go far beyond injustice, reason and mind. Many times, love means giving people more than what corresponds to them.

It is not just about controlling your mind in meditation for a few minutes. You have to meditate before and after each word you utter and each action you execute. Meditate whether you are just, unjust or loving in each situation. Each time life asks you for an answer, these three forms of acting will be in front of you. To be loving is perfect, to be just is good and to be unjust is not so good. But if there is something truly harmful, that is to believe you are just and loving when you are not. Believing you are better than what you are prevents you from climbing up this three-step ladder. How will you be truly just if you already are in your opinion? Is it not already injustice to believe you are better than what you are?

If you wish to continue the journey in some way, the important thing was, is and will be *consciousness*. This means that one day you can perceive the nature of your actions with clarity and objectivity. May your 'I am just' or 'I am good' mental patterns do not block you from seeing when your behavior is unjust. It is much more positive to admit: 'At this moment I don't have enough strength or honesty to respond in the best way so I take responsibility for the consequences of my injustice'. This apparently negative and selfish answer elevates me above my self-deceit and it is much better than drowning our own consciousness in absurd justifications. If you want to go first in the path of light, you have to become transparent —honest— so you do not create a shadow for those coming behind you.

The first figure

We must not see number 3 only as the relationship between existence and love, i.e. as the consciousness rising from them. It contributes a third concept at this point, order. If we only have two equal elements, the concept of order or alignment does not rise because, however you place the elements they will only express distance and direction but not order. Number 3 is a different case that besides expressing the previous concepts it also manifests those of alignment, closed system and stability. Two points will always be aligned between them, but three points express a special intention, they can express more concrete things. As far as stability, the ternary can express the first geometric figure and from there we can build a tripod or a table with three legs.

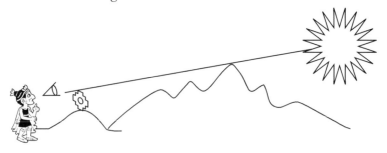

As far as alignment the ternary allowed the ancient wise ones to measure time utilizing celestial bodies. In South America, *intihuatanas* were alignment systems that had three points. A fixed central point that was usually the peak of a mountain, a second point in movement could be the Sun, the Moon or the stars and a third point could be a carved stone or a stake that the observer would stand behind. In this way, each time the Sun went back to a position aligned with the points of observation and the point of reference, they understood a year had gone by.

The trinity

I recognize and respect the right for each person to have his or her own beliefs. Even from an including optic, it is not only a right but also an obligation to express alternative forms of conceiving the sacred. I do not intend to question trinity in its 'triunity' aspect. Trinity exists in many ways in the universe. I also do not deny its existence or its reality as part of a religious system but what I cannot do is to recognize the Christian trinity in the level they pretend to place it because it omits the feminine principle.

Lets understand this well, it is not about trying to make a system prevail over another, it is about returning the feminine its sacred nature in a way that we return that same nature to matter, and in this way we can maybe reconsider our relationship with matter, women and the planet. It is more than evident to me that the deterioration of life quality and the abuse towards mother earth have a lot to do with this: a grave mistake on the origin of the divine. I am not saying because I fancy it or to try to innovate, it is enough to look at the consequences of this unusual Trinitarian patriarchal model to sense that something is not working well. The Trinitarian model exists and fits perfectly within a quaternary system.

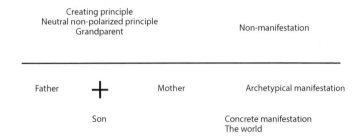

When I speak about non-manifestation, I refer to the moment previous to the *big bang*, the big crunch or any theory that wants to explain the origin of the universe. From that point manifestation starts. What is created first? Space and Time.

The figure of the grandfather-mother is key to resolve this mystery. When we say grandparent, we are referring to the undifferentiated creative principle, totally asexual, the past unity. The pure but not manifested consciousness. It is senseless to give attributes of the cause without cause to who is already sexually polarized as and energy (god father).

When unity decides to manifest it needs to split, to polarize antagonistically and complementary creating the first father and the first mother, the first couple of archetypes. In the Andean tradition: Pachamama and Pachakamaq, the mother of Space and the father of Time respectively. After the interaction and the relationship between Space and Time everything that exists is created, the dance of creation starts represented by the son. The figure is completed with the son because he is in charge of reconciling duality, of bringing together what separated, of incarnating duality, of manifesting consciousness and undergoing the experience of separation, coming back to unity.

The fact that individuals can incarnate this consciousness is part of every sacred story. At least it is one of the options. Many world traditions share this same myth that in reality is no myth but pure reality. In India it was Krishna, in the Middle East, Jesus and in America, Tunupa. And I imagine several hundred more unknown enlightened individuals born in every tradition in the world that were able to manifest the mystery of unity in this earth. This is the complete picture of the universal archetype and the model that incarnates the myth of *logos* or the cosmic Christ.

We humans are the perfect image of trinity, as much as we are a duality and a quaternary. We can totally agree in this but we disagree in the values or concepts we assign to each Trinitarian aspect. In any case I find *Satchitananda*, the Vedic conception of trinity in the human being much more balanced. *Sat* is 'existence', *chit* is 'consciousness' and *ananda* is mostly translated as 'infinite well-being' but we could simply call it love.

Pressing followers of any devotion to abandon reason to transcend the mind has been an almost essential mechanism used by many groups and religions. Even though this device is valid, we have to consider that part of the reason they ask us to abandon is to obtain a full benefit. To transcend the mind and at the same time get rid of an unnecessary belief would be twice as useful. To teach to transcend the mind over concrete and specific things like selfishness, intolerance and stinginess. Instead of smashing our mind against some dogma, I propose to offer it searching for love and service.

Grandfather-father-son and grandmother-mother-daughter are also valid triads that at some moment were an irreplaceable tool for the continuity of many initiations, both in the masculine as in the feminine lines. Jesus of Nazareth comes to teach us the mystery and the power of the cross. He does not even insinuate the Trinitarian dogma at any point. This concept appears several centuries later. We are also not interested in discussing if it was copied from or inspired by previous traditions like the Babylonian where the triad father-mother-son is still clear; or the Egyptian where the feminine figure disappears coinciding with politics of patriarchal edge. The archetypical trinity has an intrinsic and unavoidable value. We can find it and recognize it in innumerable triads. The Trinitarian Judeo-Christian model precisely leaves aside the balancing element, the complement.

A second opposite version where the masculine principle was omitted would have been equally arbitrary. It would have also motivated my irate protest.

Where we come from and where we are going

Part of the unarguable success of the psychological meaning of the Christ myth can be understood better taking a look at thousands of years of human evolution. When we speak of a cyclic time many are confused and think of a circular time in which events repeat. This is never so. The cyclic time is actually a spiral. Events are not repeated but can be very much alike when they pass through a similar point of the spiral. There are cycles that allow us to recognize certain similarities with situations of the past. In these years we have been approaching to what we call a *point of phase*, which is the end of a great cycle and the beginning of another.

At the dawn of humanity, the I was collective and tribal because it was the only way to survive, but the evolutionary plans of creation included the process of individuality. So that man had to evolve from the collective I to the individual I and enrich himself with this experience. There are some that even think that the introduction of alcohol was part of this necessary evil of the consolidation of the individual I —Dionysian initiations and Bacchus cult—. We must not fall into the mistake of thinking the first collective I was good and the second individual I was bad because it would be like judging a movie without watching the end.

The end of the movie is, after the human being enriched with the development of the individual I, he returns to the bosom of his community to enrich it with the experience of individuality. In the Hindu version it would be something like ending the experience of separation. The whole process of individuation concludes with the understanding of duality and its simultaneity. Only then it is possible to live and work for and from a community without entering into conflict with the natural appetites of a non realized I.

It is frequent to find the fact, specially among some scholars of the Andean world, that every non collective manifestation is judged as selfish or even worse as 'western' without understanding that the historic and evolutionary process as a humanity means, starting from collectivity, to achieve individuation and come back to the community enriched with this experience. We must reach a point to express ourselves alternative and simultaneously, now as a group, now as an individual and contemplate in this event the meaning of parity and complementarity.

The incarnation of the Christ myth is a true milestone in the history of humanity because far beyond its religious connotation, it expresses a real and concrete fact that is the incarnation of the verb, the 'I am', the son of the collective man. In this way humanity reaches its intense desire to capture its longing for individuation through a universal and venerable figure. Starting at this moment, this process of individuation accelerates until it is exaggerated and distorted in the exaltation of idols in modern culture, true and supreme models of selfishness with some honorable exceptions.

We are one step away from achieving this and one step away from loosing it. Will the untamable selfishness win or will we be able to enjoy all the joy and blessings that unity brings? It depends on our effort to achieve consciousness; it depends on each and every one of us.

Consciousness

People usually ask: 'is it bad to eat meat? Does it make me less spiritual?' I don't believe this to be a good approach; my work is not writing an almost infinite list of what is good and what is not. I am here to speak about consciousness among other things.

What do you think about when you have a piece of meat in front of you? Are you capable of visualizing that animal alive in front of you and you slitting its throat and cutting a piece of it? Can you imagine thousands of acres of Amazonian forest cut down, millions of animals, plants and insects that lived there all turned into ashes and into pastures for cows that will become stakes and burgers? If you can be conscious of all this and admit that at this stage of your evolution you cannot do without killing innocent lives and eat them; if you can be conscious of all this I believe you do deserve to eat a piece of meat, because killing all those cows and cutting down forests is not as serious as killing your consciousness, drowning it in the immediate vision and hiding in your schemes: 'do I even kill the cow? do I cut down the forest?'. If you are not capable to see beyond the four walls of your little house you will not even be able to dream about walking a sacred path where there is no good or evil, only consciousness.

We have to understand there exist a cosmic order and natural priorities we must recognize and respect as human beings and as a society, instead of going around listening to the intelligent argumentations of our little mind.

The ladder of three steps: sex, money and power

One of the most important teachings I remember is that the human being is conditioned by these three great motivations. The relationship with them must be totally resolved before feeling and enjoying the treasures of the heart. The person that is training to conduct others through a sacred path has to become extremely vigilant in his relationship to these three points. He cannot take advantage of the sexual or economic or social. If he did, he simply would not have understood the lesson yet and would be causing great damage to himself and others. Someone that abuses sacred plants or any other power for their benefit still remains in a very primitive state seeking for basic pleasures, even if they stated the contrary. Things are so distorted; a few months ago in a jungle city famous by its shamans I met a German young woman writing a thesis on sexual harassment in ayahuasca ceremonies. I fully honor and thank my human condition and within it my capacity to be outraged with those shamans that play with sex, money and the power of others.

We arrive at the vibration of the heart after overcoming the temptations, the lies and the self-deceit that come from sex, money and power. And in our sacred path we transform them into sacred sex, sacred money and sacred power. How to know if they are sacred? Simple. To follow a sacred path is the triumph over selfishness. If what I do I do from the ego and for the ego, it will never be sacred. The one who walks a sacred path only thinks about common good, about family; from his little family to the family of all that exists.

Money has become gradually more important in this planet. The search for material satisfaction and comfort has become an obsession in the dominating culture. The ethical border moves every time some countries or human beings want to step forward in their development. The legal forms to obtain money have become outrageously hypocritical and consciousness nullified to a point of not seeing the damage inflicted on the planet and ourselves.

We have built a world economic order based on the cruelest injustice, and the measure each one benefits with this system is directly proportional to the size of their silence or their discrepancy. And since the most affected ones do not have the means to claim their rights, everything stays in nothing.

All the wealth stolen by the empires from their colonies, the ridiculous prices the US government bought-stole the lands from the native Americans, the thousands of tons of silver and gold stolen from Bolivia and Peru killing millions of beings in the mines, all the rest they stole from Africa and Asia, all that initial stealing helped them to capitalize and achieve a great exploitation technology. They live off of royalties now. The robbery and abuse from colonial times seem far away. Those responsible do not exist any more but their fortunes remain. That same stolen gold is sold today in Wall Street. The lands of indigenous people now are highly priced but they do not belong to them anymore.

I know that very few people are interested in admitting that the system that gives us the comforts we are enjoying has an obscure origin, however honest you believe is your way to make money. Even if you do not want to see it, this generosity life gives you because 'God bless America' is nothing but the other side of the coin of all the suffering and scarcity in more than half of the world. Of course you will say: 'I didn't do things this way'. But how comfortable is it to benefit thanks to so much injustice. You find it very difficult to see, to admit it is really uncomfortable and painful but it is a million times more painful to kill your consciousness so that your selfishness survives. It is easier to close this book, to say 'I am not to blame for this' and go to the fridge and get a beer or light some incense. At that exact moment a child is dying of thirst in Africa and another of malnutrition in the Andes. Why? Because they are not as intelligent as you or as brilliant as you? Or maybe for their bad *karma*? You are not to blame but you are responsible, we are all responsible. Love hurts and consciousness hurts. Consciousness that does not hurt is not consciousness.

We not only become conscious of the beauty and of how wonderful existence is but also of the pain of that whole other part of the great human family that is only conscious of suffering and scarcity. Our only honest way out is to admit the cruel injustice of the system, to recognize both you and I benefit from knowing how to move around in it and starting there, work arduously to change it and mitigate the pain of our brothers and sisters. It is not only a matter of loving others anymore.

Human selfishness and their insatiable search for comfort are seriously affecting the planet. We keep treating her like a thing, not like a mother and our vanity and stubbornness impede us to see what relation there is between our lifestyle and the destruction of earth. What is the relation between a million tons of detergent thrown to the sea with brushing my teeth with mint toothpaste or that I wash my hair with the latest shampoo? How much does it affect if I drink a Coca Cola? What does my Caribbean vacation have to do with global warming? Nowadays everything has to do with everything. The week following the attack to the twin towers, flight suspended almost all around the world was enough to bring down the rate of global warming. There is no worse blind as the one that does not want to see. In these times we cannot speak of religion without speaking of ecology. We are paying the consequences for allowing those that divorced spirit from matter to deceive us. They elevated the spirit and condemned matter. Now it is time to put things in their place. Spirit and matter together in Time and Space, here and now. Where are all those great spiritual leaders in the struggle to stop this madness? Why they are never seen in a Greenpeace boat trying at least to save a whale or trying to stop a bombing?

We arrive to the third step. We can renounce illicit sex and money but power is a gem with many facets. It is much more subtle than the two previous ones. Only the most absolute and strict sincerity can take us beyond power. An ancient Iranian teaching says there are two types of perverse beings. One kind is found in bars and clubs and it is enough to not frequent those places to not run into them. But there is another kind that likes to hide in temples and schools and repeat great teachings taken from books. These are the most dangerous ones.

You can renounce sex and money but the need of admiration and recognition —specially after so much 'sacrifice'— can become somehow obsessive and compulsive. Your mind can take you to live the greatest sacrifices and austerities with the only goal of seeking recognition in the circles where you move. It is the same mental pattern of self-admiration. Just like some get respect and admiration showing off the latest most expensive car, some get it showing off the greatest austerity.

Power is the last test of the mind: to change the power of reason for the power of love. We have to yield at some moments and loose reason to find love. Love becomes reason and reason is love. The heart becomes the mind and the mind becomes heart. In the words of Cesar Calvo: 'The air becomes water and water becomes air'.

When we exhaust the desire to prevail, to win arguments, to get honored and recognized by our altruism, by our 'spirituality', to be thanked for renouncing couples, family, money —even if we belong to institutions with millions in the bank— when we renounce enlightment itself, then we are beyond power, the power of the ego and we see things exactly as they are without any personal interest to make them what we want them to be.

They say that at a very advanced age the Buddha called two of his favorite disciples and told them: 'I will part soon and before I go I want to grant each of you a wish. Meditate on it all day and come back here tomorrow'. Next day they came back and sat with the Buddha who asked the first one: 'dear son, what do you wish the most?' He answered: 'Master grant me enlightment'. And the Buddha said: 'may it be so according to your understanding' Then he looked at the other one and asked: 'tell me son, what do you wish the most?' The disciple answered: 'Master, I want to stay on earth and serve, spreading your teachings until every being is enlightened'. This way the Buddha showed the true nature of his teaching, compassion, which is not limited to or stopped by enlightment. Love is the supreme end.

The sacred family

All these years working with serious people that really want to heal and be happy, the most recurring theme is the relationship with the family. People that are 40 or 50 years old still do not forgive the 'mistakes' their parents made during their upbringing or the 'offenses' they were subjected to throughout their life. Another great problem is to have a deeply wounded child by multiple circumstances. The high percentage of children that were victims of abuse even by their own relatives is amazing. This will never be clear in statistics because the great majority of abuses are never reported. Working with ayahuasca in very deep levels, people realize of the need to free themselves from those tremendous pains in order to continue walking and recover the joy of living.

We should say like psychiatrists say: 'it all started in childhood'. And that is the pure truth. We find adults daily that still have not forgiven their father or mother and they keep blaming their parents for everything that happens and happened to them. We have to understand that this chain of suffering comes from the missing link. I am absolutely convinced that each father and each mother do everything possible from their wisdom or ignorance to give their children wellbeing. I will never question their intention even if the results are catastrophic. If they had been better, they would have done better. Not only we have to care for our children but specially respect them. What is good for me might not be good for them. The only thing that is certain is they gave us all the love they could. Maturity and mental clarity in human beings start when they stop blaming their parents, life and the universe for all they gave or did not give them. We have to cut this chain of reproaches and grudges and work to not repeat history.

Before giving a step in a sacred path it is indispensable to heal the relationship with our parents because we not only owe them life itself and the gratefulness this entails, but they are our most clear models of unconditional love. Besides, the primordial energies —Pachamama and Pachakamaq— descend and ascend to us through our parents. If the relationship with our parents is blocked, what can we expect of other relationships?

The family is in crisis in the whole planet because the selfishness of human beings has never been so grand. The basic cell that forms society is sick and it is not a cancer any more, it is a metastasis. However, I am optimistic and I believe in 'miracles'. It depends on each one doing their job well. From there stems the necessity to form strong families, stable commitments to not create more unnecessary suffering.

Strangely, the use of plants of power is so wide and allows so many things that one cannot understand how they can be used both for good and for evil. As I explained before, power is neutral and it depends on who uses it and for what. This means that who decides to follow the correct path does it for love of good, even if sometimes it is the hardest and most disagreeable path. The line between good and evil is very thin, almost invisible, it is only seen with the heart; moreover, sometimes it can be straight, sometimes undulating. No one can tell you what is good, only your heart knows. But listen well to see if it is your heart or your mind speaking.

CHAPTER IV

The quadripartition

The culture of Tawantinsuyo

The word 'Tawantinsuyo' means in Quechua language 'that it has four regions' and it can be understood as the four regions of the universe. I prefer to use the word 'culture' instead of 'empire' for the following reasons. First, to speak of the Tawantinsuyo empire refers only to its last stage i.e. the Inca Empire. Second, the word 'empire' describes a political model that does not fit Andean reality. Third, Tawantinsuyo is for us admirers of this culture a cultural continuum of over 5000 years that is manifested throughout the large extension of the Andean territory where several ethnic groups shared fundamental understandings about the order of things and the relationships of human beings with the cosmos for millennia. Finally, when we refer to the Tawantinsuyo as a culture we are trying to say it is not a closed subject. The last pages have not been written yet. Each person that today still cultivates and shares the values and understandings that originated this culture is preparing the terrain for the next version of the Tawantinsuyo: the fifth Tawantinsuyo, the universal Tawantinsuyo.

The majority of modern scholars point out four great moments in Andean history or, put another way, four great Tawantinsuyos. With this we do not intend to take away importance from all the other great cultures that developed at and around the same time and that shared the same concepts and basic values.

The first great Tawantinsuyo corresponds to the Formative period. The discovery of the Caral citadel in the coast of Lima opened a new chapter in our history. Discoveries like the *quipu* found in one of the chambers allow us to talk of a cultural project of five millennia. The second great expression of Tawantinsuyo corresponds to the Chavin period. Thanks to their stone and ceramic crafts it is possible to identify the basic symbols that express this continuity. They are the *chacana* and the stair and the spiral, both recognized and consecrated all through the Americas. The third moment of Tawantinsuyo is called Tiawanako-Wari. Here we observe quite a mature culture. We find an organization in it with capacity to make great works that could take more than one century. They built palaces, cities, fortresses and roads that the Incas continued to work on. The fourth Tawantinsuyo corresponds to the Inca period. It is the highest expression of this culture with abundant proof of having capitalized all the advances, scientific and cultural findings of their predecessors. Metal smiths from the north and weavers from the south had a date in the great political and religious capital of South America. They showed an organizational capability never seen before, as much as the planning and execution of monumental master pieces. Each of these moments of cultural expansion we call Tawantinsuyos had its own reasons of time and circumstances to appear and disappear. As I pointed out at the beginning, this is not a history book and for this reason I will not comment on historical aspects widely explained in other works.

The power of the symbol

There are many discoveries of modern science that confirm the wisdom of ancient peoples. One of them is the work of professor Emoto, a Japanese scientist that photographed the molecular pattern of water under different influences. He placed stickers in the bottles with words like 'thanks', 'love' and 'hate'. The experiment was concluding. The bottles that had stickers with nice words showed very beautiful and harmonious molecular patterns whereas the others expressed chaotic and unpleasant images. His theory speaks of the consciousness of water, of its capacity to receive information and change its molecular pattern with different graphic, auditory and other influences. His practical conclusion was that the human body, being composed 70% water is vulnerable to all kinds of influence, weather good or bad. For this reason the ancient ones paid close attention to what kind of designs they carried in their clothing. Some designs are considered medicine by many cultures of the world and others are almost neutral, but there are some that are truly negative. Even worse when designs that are tattooed in the skin.

This knowledge of the influence of symbols is part of the secret of ancient tattoos. When someone tattooed a power animal or a magical symbol of protection, they knew what they were doing. Nowadays this meaning is completely lost and people get anything tattooed, even truly horrendous images without caring about the meaning and ignoring how these images affect their lives and those of others. Tawantinsuyans knew the power of symbols and made an effort to decorate their garments with adequate designs and colors in a way that when two beings encountered, they looked at each other, read and recognized each other. Words were only poetry or accompaniment. Domestic utensils and jewelry were also not decorated with random drawings following mere aesthetic patterns. The designs expressed the understanding and wisdom of each artist who was a master of the word in every sense, always trying to contribute his experience to the collective consciousness. Knowledge is in the symbol.

Essence and form

Our mind will always be in charge of giving form whereas our love is related to essence. Taking this to a social context, we see that cultures have something central, something truly essential but it is manifested in multiple forms. These forms inevitably change and it is part of the nature of cultures to also express diversity in terms of the ancient and the modern. Ancient forms and new forms. The new branches of a tree are joined to its roots. We cannot grab an axe and destroy every new branch because we dislike it or because we think it goes against the essence. There are those that hold on to ancient forms thinking that if the form changes, the essence of the culture is totally distorted.

Forms, music, gowns, designs, colors, materials and costumes can change over centuries but if the essence does not change the culture is the same. The form of Tawantinsuyo has changed a lot in 5000 years, more so taking into account that there were many manifestations and tendencies in its core. But the essence remains to this day. In my humble understanding, the essence of Tawantinsuyo is the quadripartition together with the dualistic vision of the universe, evidently included are the including logic and trivalent thinking, however they prefer to call them.

The concept of complementary opposition has not yet been given enough importance in academic contexts and even less among the general population. It would be very positive if all the people that defend their own vision of the Tawantinsuyo reflected a bit on inclusion. Many voices are raised claiming they are the one and legitimate representatives and interpreters of the Tawantinsuyo culture. Nothing more unreal and contrary to its essence.

It is widely known that when the Tawantinsuyo conquered another ethnic group, this group was integrated, it was invited to be a part, and it was allowed to move its gods and its *huacas*. They even built temples in the city of Cusco for the most important ethnic groups. I have been conquered by the essence of this culture that is love, inclusion and tolerance. I belong to its essence even though I have my own form. I do not find it coherent to explicitly or subtlety raise racist or xenophobic arguments when history has proven how much a crime that is.

In many cases we can have the same goals but not the same motivation. This is evident in the discrepancies when it comes to what strategies to follow to achieve the same goal. It is not just about the difference in the way of acting. In this case the line that separates essence from form becomes a bit blurry, because those who believe they are struggling for essence are maybe just doing it for form. But what differentiates us the most is motivation. We can struggle from love or from hate.

The pain of an insulted and hurt people can be understood and felt. This is not only in our collective memory but also in our cellular memory. But to plant the seed of hate and revenge is not the path to restore a culture. It is the sermon most easily spread but it is not the vision that heals. It is the one that sickens and if it would finally triumph, we would be killing the essence of that for which we struggle. The essence of our culture is love and tolerance. Our love cannot be restored hating those that took it away from us. For the liberation of our peoples, we can struggle from hate towards the 'enemy' or from love for our people. The latter is the only option for me.

An ancient Sufi story tells of two worriers, one Christian and the other Muslim that were fighting near Jerusalem. It was a combat of honor so there was a third party observing without intervening. When the Muslim finally defeated the Christian, he put his sword on his opponent's neck and gave him a few seconds for his last prayer. Then the Christian worrier spat on the Muslim's who that hesitated for a few seconds but then released him and let him go. The man observing the fight asked him: 'why did you let him go?' The worrier answered: 'because at that moment I hated him'.

The grandparents saw the future

It is not difficult for many people that had the opportunity to experience other states of consciousness —either with plant teachers or other techniques— to believe that beings could exist with the capability to see the future. I do not think at all that the future is determined but I believe there are tendencies and probabilities for something to happen and people exist with a special gift to see images of these possibilities. It is an evident fact and it almost happens daily to have intuitions of things that will happen which many times surprise us in their accuracy. The question is how far ahead these images are. A month? A year? Some centuries? I do not particularly put a limit to them. However, thousands of years ago there could have been people that in special states of consciousness foresaw this chaotic civilization. At what we call the dawn of civilization they opted for a different model of life, for a different way to do things and to conduct societies through other paths. The great difference is that back then they saw the possibilities and they chose afterwards, whereas now the western world has created an immense snowball, a giant avalanche called 'every man for himself' without the option of someone stopping ahead even for a second to wonder where we are going.

I am not against technology or progress; but at this price? The way things are, all the good and beautiful things brought by our precious technology do not justify either the pain or the damage we are inflicting on mother earth. The question is: did the ancient ones see this disaster? I think they did. They did see it and opted for other paths, with no writing and no wheels. It is not they did not write because they could not but because they did not want to. I have learned much more from the symbols than from so much useless wording. I acknowledge that maybe we have lost much of that capacity to read and write those symbols. The true teaching cannot be given just in words; the symbol brings the complete message to us.

The great blessing

We have stopped *feeling* the damage we cause, we ignore the sacredness of other reigns of nature and we believe we are the kings of creation, that we are the center of the universe and that everything is here to serve us. With so little sensitivity it is impossible to define where is the limit of the technology we can use. At the moment a human being stops *feeling*, he

CHAPTER IV | The quadripartition

literally looses half of his condition and becomes half human. He thinks but does not feel. Lets always remember that having emotions is not the same as feeling. To feel is to LOVE. Lets reflect whether this whole approach about our role on earth has or does not have a religious origin with terrible consequences.

Are we guilty of this? Never guilty, always responsible. Lets leave guilt for those that like to punch their own chests and lets ask the father of rationalism Descartes, what was he feeling when he said 'I think, therefore I am'. Lets move further back in time when Moses himself in his version of paradise tells that his God expels man and woman with a triple curse. God Cursed woman, earth and man. I dare to quote literally this passage of the *Genesis* from the bible, because I think this text is the beginning of the great confusion on which the whole Judeo-Christian culture is built:

> And God said: who taught you that you were naked? Have you eaten from the forbidden tree?
> And the man answered: The woman you gave me as companion gave me from the tree and I ate.
> Then Jehovah God Told the woman: What have you done? And the woman said: the snake tricked me and I ate.
> And Jehovah God told the snake: For what you have done, you will be cursed among all beasts and among all animals of the country; on your chest you will crawl and you will eat dust every day of your life.
> And I will put enmity between you and the woman, and between your seed and her seed; she will hurt your head and you will hurt her foot.
> God said to the woman: I will multiply greatly the pains in your pregnancy; you will bear children with pain; and your desire will be for your husband and he will posses you.
> God said to the man: for how much you obeyed the voice of the woman, and you ate from the forbidden tree when I told you 'you will not eat from it'; cursed will be the earth for your fault; with pain you will eat form it every day of your life.

As a father of a large family, the first thing that comes to mind is that I always try to be attentive to the proportion between fault and reaction. This triple curse —for life—, just for not obeying once is a little out of proportion. My children would not accept such injustice. Second: I know few parents capable of putting a curse on their children. I find it difficult to imagine such a cruel God: increasing birth pains, condemning to suffer in order to earn the daily bread, putting a curse on mother earth. Third: to this day we pay the consequences for the ideological contraband contained in this little passage.

I believe very few people have pondered on the effects these curses have on the collective unconscious. On women mostly guilt. This curse makes women unconsciously carry the weight of having introduced evil into existence. 'It is my fault they expelled us from paradise'. All this abnegation sometimes pushed to martyrdom and many scenes of self-torture bearing truly inhuman loads —beatings and abuse at home— have their origin in this unconscious belief that they have to suffer to pay for some guilt. Women bear the heaviest load, at least in 'third world' societies. Through abuse we are killing that kindness, that capacity of sacrifice that creators placed in the feminine. The permanent reproach toward women for having lost paradise lives in the unconscious of men. For this reason, every time we are not doing well at work or we believe life is exaggeratedly unjust or when we get a flat tire we unconsciously know who to blame. Who is to blame for all this? Now you know.

'For how much you obeyed the voice of the woman, and you ate...' Symbolically, the woman and the feminine represent the intuition, the heart. The unconscious message is: 'do not listen to your intuition or your heart, obey only your mind'. On the other hand I do not think putting a curse on work and even less on farm work comes from divine inspiration. Work is a blessing. If I don't work I don't feel happy.

On what minds has this culture been built? We gave these people the power and the credibility. Now it is time for us to revise everything and everyone until we find the moment we as humanity stopped feeling. I think and I feel, therefore I insist. As a complement to this triple curse, I propose a triple blessing for women, men and the earth. (Even though we are a little disobedient sometimes).

The religion of reality

One of the greatest achievements of Tawantinsuyo culture was to not create a religion disconnected from reality but completely intertwined with it. The main figures of their imaginary —earth, Sun, Moon, mountains, our *Apus*, rivers, lagoons, thunder, water springs, *pukios*— express a very high understanding in which the necessity to invent deities or to speculate about their relations is little or non-existent. Having had the sensitivity to feel and understand the power and energy of these forms of life speaks highly of the grandparents. Nobody made me believe in the *Apus* but after a few years living at the feet of these giant mountains of amazing beauty, I was able to interpret them as a great power. Something so beautiful is necessarily powerful and holds great energy that speaks, inspires and communicates many things. One can understand and feel the tenderness of the Sun as a great father giver of life and the earth as our great mother that supports and sustains us. It is a matter of sensitivity or level of consciousness —which in the end is the same— whether you give it intelligence, life and spirit to the Sun, the earth or the mountains.

I imagine some men at obscurantism times —many with a scarce vocation and little understanding— carrying heavy crosses, dogmas, demons and fears, arguing among them whether inhabitants of America had a soul or not. To run into a religion without dogmas or speculations and people that simply worshiped reality must have been an overwhelming experience for them.

In the Andes, the process of creating a religion through 5000 years of history, agriculture and cities with flowering commerce followed a very different course than in Europe. Religion was not either dogmatic nor centralist here. When we speak of

Tawantinsuyo we speak of religion as the sum of rites and understandings that allow man to relate with the sacred.

Throughout this cultural continuum the peoples of Tawantinsuyo took the solid bases of their predecessors and continued building upon them until the time of the invasion. It is almost comical how modern theology pretends to undervalue the wisdom of the ancient ones calling pantheism —'the totality of the universe is the only God'— to the simple fact of honoring reality. The wise ones from other times, our grandparents —honest people— taught us to love reality, to honor what gives us life on all levels and to consider ourselves parts of this great family of existence, not its center or the main object of worship.

The whole mystery is resolved when we recover the capacity to feel, not the emotive function of the mind. From this moment on there is no point in deceiving or self-deceiving or in trying to intellectually prevail over others. We loose the taste for lying and inventing a religion saying it is not our creation but a divine revelation. Religion —seen as a system or ethical rules and agreements to establish norms of relation— is positive and has a very important function in society. But when these agreements only work to manipulate people and take advantage of them it is not religion anymore but vile exploitation. Each society has the right to establish these agreements for its benefit and with these norms conduct their members through a truly evolutionary path of love and respect.

The mind of human beings continues to evolve. It will be increasingly more difficult to conduct or manipulate them through dogmas. The present time asks for a reconsideration of what we understand by 'God'. I remember when I was a child; each Christmas my brother and I wrote our letters asking for gifts and hang them on a tree for Santa Claus to pick them up. Years later we accidentally discovered all the letters in a drawer and that was the end of the beautiful myth. Nowadays many people start to notice the difference between what it means to worship a God that lives in our mind —constructed by religions, sustained only by our beliefs— and to recognize another, the true creator that exists beyond all religion and dogma. When we are children we believe certain things appropriate of that age, when we grow up life itself invites us to come closer and closer to reality.

In an ancient Andean tradition I found one of the most clear and beautiful examples of how a religion is created in a society. They say that children born with a deformity, disability or mental retardation were considered *illa*, i.e. sacred, and were seen as a blessing for the family. And in the same way when there were several ears of corn in the same husk or when animals were born with a sign that made them different, they were sacred. What a beautiful way to resolve an intense social situation: to utilize the mechanism of religion and declare these special children sacred and a blessing instead of looking at them with pity and consider them losers in our society. I do not stop being amazed by such wisdom.

The quadripartition

It is a very old concept, a reality previous to human beings, as ancient as the universe. Let us date back to the very moment of the *big bang*. It is not difficult for me to imagine these four concepts being created simultaneously: Space, Time, Energy and Matter. Curiously, one of the legends of the formation of the Incan civilization is that of the four *Ayar* brothers —number four as a formative principle—.

Like we saw at the beginning of this book, the quadripartition is the result of dividing duality. It is to my understanding the best way to understand this constructively. The ancient ones understood it in the following way: parity and complementary are not only expressed in *lloq'e-paña* —left and right— but also in *hanun-urin* —high and low—. This allows to see reality in more than two dimensions —black and white— opening the door to a completely different universe.

The first practical example that comes to my mind is the discourse of a lecturer giving a dissertation about including logic and quadripartition, and he was speaking badly of western culture without granting it anything positive. Beyond not understanding the essence of quadripartition he seemed to have the following discourse: we indigenous people are the good ones, all the rest are bad. A true Tawantinsuyo master would not put it that way but he would apply the double division: among my people there are wise ones and ignorant ones, same as with foreigners. The history of the Americas would have been very different if the ships that arrived in our shores had been loaded with musicians, poets, wise ones and true priests instead of greedy bandits.

Not all cultures gave the same importance to quadripartition but we do find important samples of this understanding since remote times. The oldest stone monument that transmits this idea is the well-known sphinx of Egypt. This monumental symbol expresses the concept of quadripartition through a mythical animal. It has a human head, the front of a lion (claws), the rear of a bull and eagle wings. In this way it expresses a being with four natures, four dimensions and four energies. This symbol was recognized and maintained by the widely spread Gnostic schools in the east coast of the Mediterranean through the end of III century of this era. In this zone is the Patmos island where John the Baptist wrote his famous *Apocalypse* evidencing Gnostic influence with the reutilization of the symbolism of the four animals.

Another culture that shows a similar understanding in its iconography is Hinduism. This concept was expressed in India with the swastika. This is also a master symbol because it shows that it is not only a cross that expresses quadripartition, but it is a cross in movement indicating whether the cross is turning clockwise or counterclockwise with the last part of the line

—the one perpendicular to the arm—. They say that thousands of years ago they used two swastikas to light the sacred fire. One laid still on a base while the other one had a piece of wood in the center working as an axis so it could turn over the one that was still that symbolized the opposite turning, the feminine part. Amazing symbolism. After spinning for a while —if it was the correct wood and very dry— the sacred fire ignited, the union of the masculine and the feminine.

Other cultures left many samples from cave paintings to stone engravings allusive to quadripartition but mentioning the main ones is enough. This understanding was also among the first European cultures, shown in the following engraving:

The labarum, millenary Cantabrian symbol from the north of Spain.

But let us return for a moment to ancient Egypt where one of the most skillful strategies is plot to make a piece of knowledge eternal. In the same way I think our American grandparents could see the future, I also think the Egyptians were pretty advanced with this science. Not only they defied time building such stone monuments but they came up with an amazing game where all their wisdom is concealed in case one of those crazy people —the ones we nowadays call heads of state— decided to bombard it one day. That is how Tarot is born. Foreseeing that maybe future generations would not be very attracted to virtue, they bet to vice and fraud. Success! The game of cards was not forgotten. I imagine that very few of the enlightened card players in Las Vegas have any idea of this sacred origin. What is nowadays left of its original symbolism is very little: the four suits of cards and the images of the king, the queen and the jack. The major Arcanums were eliminated. This is a version of the Tarot that suffered total distortion. The main trunk that has its roots in Egypt was left intact. The ancient ones captured in a series of prints not only the understanding of quadripartition but the whole archetypical manifestation. Afterwards it spread around Europe with the gypsy tribes traveling from the Orient. The essence of this encrypted knowledge is precisely the understanding of quadripartition.

However, it is essential to mention that the version that arrives in Europe from faraway Egypt has an illustrious intermediary that adds valuable contributions in many ways. We are referring to the Hebrew people. During their historic stay in Egyptian lands both cultures were mutually influenced and gave place to one of the most interesting social experiments in the history of humanity. We must not forget that Moses himself tells of his real origin, he was a Hebrew child adopted by the daughter of a Pharaoh and then raised in the Egyptian court as a true prince. Some people believe this happened and some don't. One version tells that prince Moses was originally Egyptian and due to deep discrepancies with the dominating theology he decided to initiate an adventure beyond imagination. Aware of the traditional Hebrew tendency towards monotheism he rehearses an amazing synthesis: the understanding of quadripartition of the Egyptian people applied in its aspect of quadriunity with the conception of one God. Evidently, there are many things he does not tell to the Hebrews like for example the meaning or the reason for the four letters that form the word god.

The dynamic law of transformation or the wheel of medicine

In the Tarot of Marseilles, one of the most famous in medieval Europe, we find not just the original Egyptian symbols but a version with European images and the Hebrew alphabet in the 22 prints. From there we infer that the main quaternary, i.e. the four letters that represent the code that deciphers all the symbology of the cosmic law expressed in the Tarot surprisingly 'coincides' with the four letters in the Hebrew word to name god: IHVH. As you might know, no vowels were written in ancient Hebrew, which generated all these possible readings: Ihevhe, Iavhe, Yave, Jehova.

We can find an immediate relationship between this cycle of transformation and our solar year. The two solstices and equinoxes form a sequence of four movements that is one of the first references to the concept of cyclic counting. It was also one of the great advances in every civilization to become aware of these annual periods to achieve the notion of time and be able to be adequately oriented, particularly with the advent of agriculture. In this way they clearly identified four principal moments through solar observatories. The summer solstice that marks the northernmost point of the sun; the equinox that marks the central point in the itinerary; then the winter solstice that marks the southern point; and finally the equinox again marking the central point. I find an amazing 'coincidence' between the repetition of two central points like the equinoxes and the repetition of the two letters H in the dynamic law of transformation (IHVH).

The name of God for the Hebrews was not in reality the name of a divine character as the people interpreted. It was the name of a cosmic law, a sequence of transformation that human beings simultaneously sensed in all continents from the beginning of humanity. The ancient wise ones arrived at an understanding of quadripartition or quadriunity, and besides that they understood it is not static but it has a sequential movement. I name this sequence of four the dynamic law of *transformation.*

Among Native American peoples, there is not only knowledge of the four regions that form the universe but also that when these four directions are turning they create the wheel of medicine that permits everything to heal and be renewed. It is exactly the same understanding but in the other side of the planet. All this is evidently an attempt to interpret an abstract reality and adapt it to images and words. It is not my intention to discuss whether the wheel is the one turning or if we are the ones moving and crossing these four energies. In reality, it could be both.

I would like to show bellow the two following diagrams that express quadripartition: the system we call western —which rises from the symbolism of the Sphinx and it is later enriched with other associations in medieval Europe— and the American system.

There are more coincidences than discrepancies between these two systems, particularly taking into account that in both cases it is symbolic words that try to express a much larger reality. To continue making distances shorter, the 'North' they refer to in the western version is not the geographical north but referential, spiritual or however they prefer to call it. In the American version it is replaced by the 'East', direction of the sunrise that always symbolizes the beginning. On the other hand these two diagrams are not the only versions. I use them because I think they are the most representative. We have to take into account that the American diagram is already a unification between the 'North' and the 'South'. This has to be approached with absolute flexibility anyway. I am not saying 'this is so'. It is simply how I see it at the moment and how I think some people saw it a long time ago. And I can imagine from these pages the joy in those able to see it this way.

This is another story of migrations similar to the Hopis' and I believe they are complementary even though the way to draw them is different. I suggest starting at the same nucleus of the cross but this time our movement from one arm to the other does not go through the center but it goes directly to the next arm in a way that our itinerary draws a spiral of sorts.

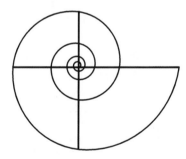

In the first direction of the diagram of the western version of the quadripartition, the 'Bull' symbolizes the start, the strength for every beginning. It is a farm animal so therefore it represents hard work, docility, humility. That is why later they associated it to the word 'Silence', because it is the first condition for who wants to learn. Silence to be able to listen but also to be able to understand what can and cannot be said.

The second direction, gate or energy is symbolized by 'Water' and 'man' —the human being— that symbolize the mind, knowledge and sensuality. The walker starts at the 'Land of the bull' and goes into 'the Water of Man' seeking for the necessary knowledge to continue the journey but in the middle of this experience he is seduced by the pleasures of the intellect and sensuality and for some time gets trapped forgetting his main objective. He does not remember anymore why he dove into that ocean of knowledge until some clues left by previous travelers make him get his memory back and resume the journey.

We continue advancing from the element 'Water' towards the element 'Fire'. What do we find further ahead? Trials, trials and more trials. It truly seems there is no path or that the path is in such bad shape that it becomes impassable at moments. But after some steps with lots of faith the path becomes visible again, not easy but visible. Exterior temperature rises but the heat generated by internal friction is much greater. Do we keep advancing even when external and internal conditions become more and more unbearable with every step or we go back to enjoying the wonderful sensuality of our watery paradises in the human sphere? Do we come back to shelter in the warm protection of the pack or face the burning destiny of all our fears, insecurities and selfishness trusting that we have a good purpose and that our will is no different than the will of the universe? This is what we will find out soon when we arrive at the gate preferred by the great mystery. We go into darkness, blackness, slander, incomprehension, disgrace, solitude and we come out with a smile and full of love.

The 'Fire' gate stands in front of us. All we truly are not is about to be destroyed. 'Want' is maybe the most precise word of the four. To complete this cycle of transformation, one has to truly WANT, let the flames of spirit embrace you and ask it to destroy all that must not continue. The 'Fire' destroys everything that is not fire. The fire of sacrifice. The fire that regenerates. The fire of the Sun. To WANT, you have to achieve a heart of a 'Lion', of a 'Puma', of an otorongo, a heart of fire. A heart that does not give up, that does not stop trying, that if it fails it tries again. That does not get tired of forgiving, of giving others and itself another chance until it is one with the 'Fire'. This is the 'Fire of the South', the southernmost point in the cross, death itself; what some would call *seol*, the place where Jesus descended to and rouse from when he died. The fire is on the altar and suddenly we discover that we are the offering. It is not a novel or a fable. It is a myth, the cosmic myth of human regeneration that becomes reality every time a human being decides to play the role.

It is a multidimensional understanding, we are describing the large wheel than can end with our physical life and also give us the opportunity —or not— to defeat death itself. But at the same time there is a million other small wheels of lesser intensity. Every time you feel the heat go up and life is testing you, it is a small wheel that is turning. Each time you find yourself before a difficult situation and lying seems to be the solution, be honest, stay firm, do not give a step back; let the wheel turn and let it transform you. The intensity will rise time after time, turn after turn until we arrive at the large wheel.

Some years ago during an ayahuasca ceremony in which I was very sad, the fire started talking to me. It asked: 'why do you suffer?' I told it I had great pain because there was so much suffering on earth. Father fire told me: 'do you want to help alleviate your brothers and sisters pain? Take this, here is the power, take it with your hands. Take my fire'. I cried even more and I felt worse recognizing I was a coward because I did not dare to receive the gift that would end so much useless suffering. I implored the fire to give me more time, I promised it I would work very hard to purify myself and try to deserve another opportunity. This is not a tale. It is possibly the most sacred thing that has ever happened to me and to this day it makes me cry every time I remember it. It put an end to my fantasies to pretend to help humanity when I was not even able yet to carry my own weight. It made me see that my worse pain was not really the 'suffering of the world' but my own inability, my own self-deceit. I don't know if I will one day be able to stand in front of that same fire and say: 'I am ready now Father'. I do not know, but I am heading in that direction.

This book is not part of a personal growth workshop where we go see if we find a more adequate partner. It is a call for those that feel the fire crackling in their heart, for those that sense great changes coming and that must prepare to face the hard trials that are coming. These changes will make many people increase their consciousness and their love but for many others it will be the loss of the little they earned.

To those that still enjoy a daiquiri in the pools of shamanic intellectuality, my regards and enjoy very much because what is next in the path is certainly no joke. I write these pages standing in front of the largest abyss I have ever contemplated. I do not know if I will live or if these pages will see the light but in any way I want to say that all of this has been written with the sincerity and the respect that my own death inspires.

I think that each being does the best they can, that nobody can jump to the next step, that each one is ok where they are and if you do not realize it now, you will eventually. Each human being is in a different process and time, in some different point of the large wheel. Use the large wheel, transform yourself with it.

Let us return to our large wheel. What is left? The 'Air', the 'Eagle'. It means to 'Dare' hold yourself with your own wings, learn to walk in the air. Nothing holds you anymore, only your own flight. Beliefs, doctrines, philosophies, paths, theories you found support in are over, including this one. None of them has any value for an eagle. Your new reality: things are and are not. Your logic is including. Your prayer: 'Everything is fine, even though sometimes it can be better.' Your love has freed itself from all conditionings; you are free of human and divine dramas. You are no longer a prisoner of the Gods and even less of good an evil. Lets be attentive, lets not loose opportunities, lets enter a wheel ever larger and more intense where the commitment is gradually larger. You will soon realize that the wheel turns, that the wheel heals, that the wheel transforms.

Before finishing, I want to comment on a practical aspect that can be of much use to better understand certain situations. Each arm of the cross of this wheel allows a possible type of situation. In total, there are four types of experiences we must go through. Four are the lessons we must learn and we can draw them as follows.

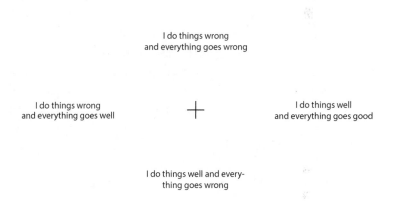

I do things wrong
and everything goes wrong

I do things wrong
and everything goes well

I do things well
and everything goes good

I do things well and everything goes wrong

This aspect of the wheel is one of the most secret and healing ones because it does not allow anyone to escape the four learnings. Everyone can remember and recognize in major or lesser degree these four possible situations in their lives. Two of them are logic and two are apparently illogic. But these two last ones are powerful medicines to understand situations that are apparently unjust. When we see so many evildoers and liars go unpunished and they apparently mock all justice, they are only experimenting a fleeting benefit. This must not mine our trust in love as the great purpose in life. And when it is our turn to face something, to do things well and everything goes wrong is a clear sign that we are in front of the 'Fire' door where all logic and all sense of justice are destroyed. Only love survives from that point. It is evidently the hardest trial; it is the mystery of the cross. Many will make fun and say that if we had done things well, what is happening to us would not happen. But when one is in that moment one knows it has to be that way.

We dare imagine unity, contemplate duality, enjoy trinity, movement, relationship... and finally arrive at the quaternary, the quadripartition... and start again, turn after turn in our sacred spiral of Space-Time-Consciousness.

In each turn I understand and feel a little more what I am doing and what is happening. The great wheel of medicine inevitably turns in spite of you and in spite of me, in spite of everything. The sacred 'animals' and the four magical words keep transforming us, the great Sphinx flies again and all this thanks to the 'primitives' that took the time to write on stone. I feel embarrassment for so much modern arrogance. I try to share the idea that from remote times there were in all continents human beings with wisdom and clarity almost unimaginable to us who understood basically the same and that even though they had to deal with the difficulties of their time, they were able to transmit the essential, the most important, the most sacred.

Imperialism and globalization

When did this globalization nightmare start? I admit that it also has some positive aspects like everything. But is it justified to completely ignore the need to protect all manifestations of the great diversity of life? It is not just a matter of demanding respect for our differences, it is about how offended cultures by abuse of power can recompose their proposal in a system of total injustice. It has to be understood that after all the imbalances and abuses caused by religious and economic imperialisms, there are forms of life —plants, animals, cultures— that are at the edge of extinction. Many unconscious minds claim that everything that does not have the strength to survive must die. I hope that the majority of people do not think in this way and reflect on what really makes us human beings.

We could think it is good to have love and compassion for all weaker forms of life. But I even find this is little consciousness. We are all responsible by being a part —actively or passively— of a system with an aggressive and overwhelming expansion that impedes the recuperation of other cultural forms. A good example of nowadays is Amazonian cultures. They have lived in harmony with their surroundings for thousand of years and they thoroughly know their environment, the Amazonian forest. This means their members are extremely cultured in their own system. Those foreign to their culture could not survive even a week in the jungle without their help. Their knowledge on botanic, entomology, biology, etc is amazing. Human beings must be considered cultured only in terms of their own culture. To look down on someone from another culture for not knowing our culture reflects very serious ignorance and arrogance.

Amazonian people need for their sustenance huge zones of virgin forests where the animals they consume —birds, fish and mammals— can live free and in good conditions. The invasions of the colonizers in the last century has reduced their territories to less than 5% sentencing all these cultures to death. We cannot say that life is simply to adapt or die. We are so blind we are incapable to acknowledge what a huge loss this represents for everybody, for life. If they disappear something will also die in us.

In 'Peruvian' and 'Brazilian' territories there still exist a few hundred families called *uncontacted* by the modern world. They are free men and women that decided to not have contact with 'civilization', at first because they loved their way of life, their costumes, their freedom and now for survival. They love their 'wild' relationship with mother earth, to walk around the jungle almost naked, to take what the forest offers them living with an open heart receiving all the love and all the pain such a life brings. I know that many think that no human being in this century should live in this state of confusion, ignorance and misery but rest assured that the leaders of these 'primitive' societies thought the same about us after witnessing our confusion, ignorance and misery (this is a perfect example of complementary visions). In present times, these 'uncontacted' peoples live under persecution in a territory more and more limited and the governments of Peru and Brazil are not taking more appropriate measures to trace a line of protection in a map. There is no turning back for them now. Their attempts to incorporate into the modern world were always disastrous. They died by the thousands due to maladies as simple as the flu — they have no defenses against our sicknesses— and nowadays they are still victims of three great predators:

1. Timber extractors that illegally invade their territories.

2. Researchers that are behind a photograph and an article that gives them fame in academy.

3. Some evangelic sects that dedicate all their efforts to take the Gospel to the last man of the planet to save his soul without caring if they kill his body or his culture.

To what point does our exquisite society require these fine woods? To what point does our curiosity need details about their lives? When did our beautiful beliefs turn into killing weapons?

The human being and the urban being

The human being is a species that develops successfully on this planet approximately 100 thousand years ago. Some more enthusiastic people speak of almost a million years ago. But in any case, for the 5 thousand million years they say our universe is we are not very significant. Even less significant is the urban being: a much younger project, no more than 500 years old and that barely takes a defined psychological profile in the last five decades. The urban being develops and spreads at a vertiginous speed without understanding or respecting the basic laws that allow coexistence with other species. It is becoming a variation of the human kind: it gradually sacrifices more and more its capacity to feel in order to favor thinking.

Urban beings abandoned the natural, real path creating their own system with their own rules. Some really despise nature and where something green grows they try to replace with concrete. Great concentrations have been created —megalopolis of 20 million people— that favor the deterioration of both quality of life and the relationship among people. The urban way of life and economic system are not real but virtual because they are based on unlimited and inevitable consumerism and in all kinds of speculative activities. Their bases and foundations are so little real that it is not an exaggeration to compare the system of urban beings to a castle built with poker cards that will come down any second. Since the larger portion of money has been concentrated in a few hands, it is no longer enough to buy and speculate with real agricultural production; now they trade speculating on the production of the next 20 or 30 years. That is to say, they are buying coffee or oranges that will be produced in 2037.

The most alarming and dangerous thing is the grade of dependency people have with relation to the urban system that at any given moment could fail for different reasons and generate the massive destruction of the urban species. If this were to unfortunately happen, the more dependent ones would be the most affected, the ones incapable to generate their own food.

On the contrary, people, peoples and cultures that at this time are marginalized by urban species will recover their freedom.

The less dependent we are from this virtual system, the more options we will have to survive. No human being living at 5000 meters of altitude in the Peruvian Andes growing potatoes nor another one living in the Amazon rainforest, nor a Bedouin in the dessert will suffer much the chaos coming from the urban centers. If I had to measure intelligence in human beings, one of the indicators could be their degree of independence to create their own food and be able to survive causing the least damage to their environment.

I always liked the ocean very much and I felt profoundly captivated by dolphins. These magical mammals, extremely intelligent, sensitive and beautiful achieved in the ocean a degree of independence and freedom beyond all our conditionings and needs. Should we consider ourselves superior to them?

Ayahuasca medicine

Culture and medicine

Since a few decades ago anthropologists try to understand and explain the particulars of each people and culture based on their geographical environment. I recognize this is an important factor in some places more than others but in the Americas it was not just the landscape or the geography what modeled the different cultures. Peyote and mushrooms in North America and in the south *wilca*, *wachuma*, ayahuasca, tobacco and coca were the medicines that transformed the inner landscape of men who developed generation after generation an unimaginable depth in their understanding of life.

To write about the Tawantinsuyo and not write about medicines would be an unforgivable omission. However, I find it overwhelming to write about ayahuasca. Because same as we saw life as a paradox, the words I would choose for ayahuasca is 'too much'. Too much love, too much intensity, too much depth, too much clarity, too much confusion, too much strictness with some, too much tolerance with others; but my gratefulness will never be too much. In spite of ayahuasca being originally from the Amazonian region and each culture has its own name for it —from Bolivia to Venezuela— the most widely known name around the world is the Quechua word *ayawaska*.

The vine of the dead or the rope of the spirit

The word ayawaska is composed by two words: aya which means 'dead' or 'spirit' and waska which means 'rope' or 'vine'. It can therefore be translated as 'the vine of the dead' or 'the rope of the spirit'. The first thing to notice is its relation to death. Many people say that from the first time they drank — and other times after— they literally felt they 'were dying'. This is something very frequent. In fact, I felt myself more than a dozen times like I was really dying. But this journey to the border of death itself is just the closest approximation you will be able to have consciously and voluntarily to it. It is very clear that in the moment of trance nobody can convince you that you are not dying for real. It seems totally real and you have to learn to overcome that if you want to continue on this path. Not all experiences have to be mandatory 'of death'. We are talking about a very intense, special situation. The majority does not necessarily take you to this encounter with death but it does take you close enough so that afterwards you reflect on a lot of things.

Lets remember for an instant some situation in our lives that brought us close to death, like when a dear relative passes away. All the seriousness, the humility, the sincerity, the love and the pain felt in these moments leave no space for our mental patterns to manipulate us, at least for some time. This gives us the key to understand —at least a little— how and why it heals. Ayahuasca is for me a ritual of death and resurrection; it disassembles you and then it puts you back together. If we are sick —and we are all sick in fact, at least with ignorance— the most probable is to feel pain, and those final moments make us seek our errors with all sincerity and ask for forgiveness from a very deep place. There is an innate and unavoidable desire to part in peace. In the end when we are coming out of that state and we see it was a big fright we return with a calm mind —practically nullified— and a feeling of profound peace and boundless gratitude.

Is consciousness permanent?

Unfortunately it is not. It slides away like water through the fingers. I have seen cases of people that before the end of the ceremony they had fallen back into their old mental patterns, while for others the sensation of having touched the sky with their hands gradually dissolves in several days. The interesting thing is that a small light is lit within that allows you to see things that need to change urgently. Ayahuasca can show you those things but it is entirely your responsibility to make those changes or not. Lets imagine our interior as a dark room, unknown, packed with furniture and strange objects. We all want to find the door, the way out but it is difficult with so much darkness. Suddenly a small light turns on for a second and we catch a glimpse of our surroundings. Then it turns on for another second and in this way we begin to recognize the space and we seek the exit or at least the light switch. With time this level of consciousness we reached momentarily starts to be gradually more frequent and stable, at least within that undulating line that the consciousness of every human being has. Even the moments of low consciousness are not so low anymore.

There are unfounded opinions about these sacred plants voiced from ignorance. People that have never experienced them say they are drugs and therefore cannot be considered as part of a spiritual path. I totally agree with them on the latter. They are not part of a 'spiritual' path; they are a sacred path. And on the former, to call sacred plants drugs is a serious lack of respect to our culture and to our teachers. They call our medicines drugs and they call their drugs medicines, how funny. To invalidate them because they are an 'external resource' used to enhance consciousness seems to me the fruit of ignorance. Everything that creators put on earth is to give it good use and ultimately, how will you get enlightened while you still think that you and the plants are something different or that you are different from everything? Precisely, when drinking it there are moments when I clearly feel unity and ayahuasca and me are one being. Despite all the spirituality some believe they have, they are still trapped in dual logic.

In spite of all this, she gives you only one opportunity and there is no guaranty of anything. That is precisely one of the first rules we have to learn. Same as ayahuasca is itself a compound —chacruna and ayahuasca—, when the energy of ayahuasca mixes with your own energy this produces a new combination. That is why the effect will be different for each person. Thousands of books could be written but not one of them will tell you more than just one experience. Each person can talk about what ayahuasca is for him or her but no one can talk about what ayahuasca itself is. The closer we can get with words is saying it is too much. *Sinchi sinchi medicina* —'too much medicine'— the elders sang.

The mind of men wants to investigate it, define it, classify it, categorize it, predict it and the more it tries to do this the greater the disappointment they will have to bear, because it represents precisely the opposite: it is indefinable and unpredictable, it shows you the path to go and return, the path from earth to heaven and from heaven to earth, it puts above what is bellow, it puts outside what you believe to be inside, it dismisses what you think is important and it turns worthless things sacred. It can shatter your reason fifty times in one night, it can heal you, it can teach you or it can ignore you. It can show you all the truths of the universe and all the lies, it can tell you fake or true stories, it can lull you like a baby or take you to panic, to madness and then to love and from total confusion to clarity. The obvious question is then: if it is like that, why drink it? The answer cannot be given from generality; it would not be very fair. Each one will have an answer after knowing it a bit, each one will know and will feel weather to drink or not.

The path of not being

I remember the first ceremonies in 1979 very well. After drinking the first ten times I thought I understood everything. After drinking for a year I though I understood 90 % of things. After five years I thought that in reality I only understood 10%. Today, after almost 30 years I am convinced that I don't know anything and just now I understand something. Evidently, you learn something after all that time and my knowledge is larger than years ago but comparatively, it is nothing in relation to the intuition of the infinite. What has developed the most in me is not knowledge but the perception of what I do not know, the intuition of the totality.

Ayahuasca taught me that to be a true guide of ceremonies, I should not follow the path of being, but of *not being*. I understood that the more I would want to control a ceremony, the worse it would be. The path was the other way around: in each ritual, to gradually reduce the ego a bit more each time and in this way make it disappear. This is what the medicine wants, not a great personality that 'is', but a tiny ego that does not get in the way. Let the medicine work, let the medicine heal, it is the meaning of being a true channel. To know the exact moment to disappear and let her take control. In this path you have to be less in order to be more; if you want to advance, first you have to move backwards.

They say a very old man wearing rags with an air of wisdom showed up at the gate of a great palace asking for an interview with the king. They received him and let him in the throne room waiting for the king. The old man felt tired and sat down. Immediately a king servant told him he could not seat there because it was the seat of the king. The old man asked: 'who is above the king?' The servant answered: 'only god'. The old man asked again: 'and above God?' The servants smiled and said: 'nobody, above God, nobody'. Then the old man said: 'well, that's me, nobody'.

In this time everybody wants everything fast and this path is not like that. A sacred path is for life and it can take 30 years to simply discover that you don't know anything. So when people come and ask me to teach them, I ask them if they really have time to learn, because many of them imagine this can be assimilated like a technique and in a few months they will travel all around the world conducting ceremonies and getting rich doing it. When someone asks me to teach them the path of medicine and tells me they want to conduct ceremonies, I tell them that many years could go by from the formal request until I could give them the blessing to do it. They look at me then like saying: 'why so long?' and they go search for someone else that will initiate them as shamans in three months.

There are those of us that followed the teachings of a master for years —traditional training, fasts and months of dieta— and those who took the three-month course. However, the medicine is so generous that it allows healing to arrive through these not so clear channels to many people because there is great necessity. Even so, it is pathetic for these reckless people, because there is not a more disagreeable and precarious role than that of an imposter. The image of people invited to a very beautiful house comes to my mind. The guests are received by someone elegantly dressed who invites them to come in, they praise the house and ask him if he is the owner. He replies with a smile, he does not say yes or no but intentionally lets people believe he owns it. The beautiful house is the house of the grandparents, the tradition. The person receiving them is the guide of ceremony, the doorman. He is just the caretaker, not the owner. The house belongs to the medicine, she is the owner and this must not be hidden. The doorman must have said 'I am just the caretaker, the house belongs to my grandparents but please come in and enjoy yourselves'. The true power belongs to the medicine, not to the facilitator.

Ayahuasca can be capable of healing you from the most strange and complicated diseases both physical and mental and it can dazzle you with the vision of all its splendor, but the one that does not know much can believe this wonder comes not from the medicine but from the person conducting the ceremony. And if this person does not have the honesty to put things clearly, he becomes a usurper. He is stealing the merit from its true owner. Even worse, when people that are absolutely grateful for their liberation or healing fall in the hands of bad shamans, they are easy preys of all kinds of sexual and profit abuse. For this reason it is important to have serious training, with a supervision that avoids this to become a business and stops being the sacred path it has always been.

On another hand, the short-sightedness of those that do not see the importance of belonging to a tradition, of feeling grateful and protected by being connected to a true linage, it is not but a typical expression of the western mind whose understanding about it is practically non-existent. As much ayahuasca as they drink, they will not change if they do not learn that the number one lesson is respect. Someone trained in a sacred path does not pull a leave without asking for permission, does not collect a stone without thanking, does not take a life if it is not necessary and if it is, he prays a lot for that life. He does not take over rites and instruments or sacred songs without having received permission. Everything has life and because of that everything is sacred, stones, plants, animals, humans. Like a great chief said: 'earth does not belong to man, man belongs to earth'. We can also look at it in the opposite way: everything belongs to me, therefore I look after it and respect it; the water belongs to me, the air belongs to me. I do not believe I am the owner of anything but I also believe I am the owner of everything.

The two most important things to learn in this life are asking for permission and thanking. The day when we can remember at every single moment that this teaching hides even in our breath, we will have achieved the memory. To feel we are asking for permission to exist when we inhale and to feel gratefulness for life when we exhale. That simple, that simple.

Sacred plants are true teachers of the vegetal kingdom capable of transmitting great knowledge. These 30 years taking them have been for me like being under the instruction of a great master. A science very difficult to understand for average modern humans was developed by the old inhabitants of the Americas. By ingesting these plants they achieved a profound degree of introspection that allowed them access to concrete and 'scientific' information —if called that— about many aspects, but mainly oriented to resolve health issues which have always been a priority need.

Collective consciousness

Ayahuasca is a beverage composed by two plants: chacruna and ayahuasca which gives the medicine its name. In the book *The cosmic serpent* by Jeremy Narby, the following question is raised: how could they find which one inhibits a hormone that impedes the assimilation of Dimethyltryptamine (DMT) among 70000 major plant species? Science has demonstrated how our thoughts can modify not only the chemistry of our body through the regeneration of hormones and different substances but also the molecular patterns of water. Many Amazonian cultures knew this since thousands of years ago. Because of that they pray on or they *icarear*[2] the medicines before taking them with the intention to harmonize them.

---

2   Icarear is a verb derived from icaro, sacred ayahuasca song. There is a difference between the act of singing and the act of icareando which has a quality practically impossible to describe in words. But that has a true magical quality.

How did these 'primitive' beings obtain all this wonderful and surprising botanical, entomologic and biologic knowledge? This is our hypothesis: all vegetable, animal and mineral species have a certain level of consciousness. Expanding Jung's theory on the human collective unconscious, where the exchange of information among all kingdoms of nature and among all its species is real and demonstrable. It would seem that the human being is the only species that has this relative individual consciousness whereas other species only have it in a collective way.

In stories of ayahuasca experiences people usually say a serpent spoke to them, that a stone confided a secret or that a plant showed them what it is for. I do not doubt this information can be real but the trap about its truthfulness can be in the capacity each ayahuasca master has to connect in a truly profound level of their being with another consciousness, where his mind does not intervene with ridiculous imaginations.

People usually ask me if I am a healer. I do not like to be labeled with any word. I pray for people to heal and for the medicine to heal them, and sometimes they heal. Like a naturist key principle says: 'the therapist accompanies you in the process while nature heals you'. It is also important to understand what is sickness. Sickness is neither a divine punishment nor solely the intrusion of a virus in your system. If our energy is well, our immune system must have enough strength to reject any sickness. But if our energy is blocked or divided, this manifests many times with pathologic symptoms. The body expresses that something is not good, that we must change an attitude or a thought, that we have resentment or something to forgive. Sickness is just the symptom of something deeper. Sometimes, if you heal someone who has not yet understood why he or she is sick, you are not doing him or her any good. This is one of the greatest kindness of ayahuasca; she tells you where you error, your pain and your sickness really are.

He died very healthy

They say that a very sick person arrived at the home of a very famous healer deep in the Amazon jungle. The healer looked at him and simply shook his head while smoking his big pipe. A week later he was telling: 'A very sick man came last week, I sucked from his head, I sucked his chest and I sucked his back[3], I extracted all the evil stuff, I left him very healthy. The man died tree days later but he died very healthy.'

The exact distance

Many years ago in a ceremony I was reflecting on the harmony of the celestial bodies, true colossus floating and dancing to the rhythm of life. I understood that what we call magnetism or gravity here on earth is simply called love in the universe. Love is the exact distance that makes us feel attracted to everything, but without leaving our own orbit to keep maintaining the harmony of the whole. If we were conscious of our responsibility in all our relationships and we adequately fulfilled our role, we would find the exact distance with everything. It is not always about being all together and mixed up until we asphyxiate. The universe teaches us to find the correct distance in each of our relationships. It is the perfect example that reconciles our destiny as individuals with our collective experience. Love or exact distance express in very strange ways. I had to tell a person once —certainly joking— that my love for her grew proportionally to the distance between us.

Speaking of the cosmic dance, we cannot leave celestial music with no mention. What role do sacred songs —*icaros*— play in a ceremony? I will speak about them first. They are the traditional songs that ayahuasca healers use in their ceremonies. There are various types. There are *icaros* to call the spirits of plants, to call

---

3 Sucking is a technique that some Amazonian healers use to extract disease and maladies.

protector spirits; also to invoke the spirit of an animal, vegetal or mineral, or any entity of nature. Some come just from human inspiration whereas others are truly the sound expression of the spirit they represent. These are without doubt the most powerful ones. But the true power lies more in the relationship between the healer and his song than in the *icaro* itself. *Icaros* reveal themselves almost always during 'dietas' and they demand a high price in effort, austerities or fasts in order for them to have true power or capacity to heal.

Repeating the *icaro* of any master makes no sense if it was not obtained correctly in the first place —with proper permission— and second, if the person did not 'diet' adequately. Another very important thing is to understand that even if all the requisites are met, the main thing is the state of consciousness one sings from. This is essential for me. To sing a sacred song —even if it is 'correctly' performed— will not have the same effect if sang from an ordinary state of consciousness or from another state of expanded consciousness. The where, the when and the why always have to be respected.

Music is essential in the type of ceremonies I do. During the first hour when the first effects of the medicine start, it is mainly the beginners who experiment their own inner chaos. Without the help of the music this state would be almost unmanageable. Music plays a role of ordering, it proposes an equilibrium, a harmony that when it is correctly directed it moves opening a path and giving solution to those very intense moments. The songs I use in ceremonies are poems that invite us to reflect on life and our path, touching very deep emotions in participants.

The distance between each note is not something arbitrary; it also represents the exact distance that exists between different vibratory levels. Even though this is not all, it is very important to sing in tune because tuning represents the respect for the exact distance and this brings harmony. Out of tune represents chaos. When singing in a ceremony surrounded by people hyper sensitized by the medicine, we are not only transmitting a song but all our life, all our clarity or our confusion, our truth or our lie. Because of the levels of sensitiveness we work with it is a very delicate matter.

'Dieta'

It is part of the traditional training of any ayahuasquero apprentice and also a part of the whole healing process in the Amazonian medical system. It basically consists of abstaining from certain foods and substances during a period of time. Mainly one has to stop eating salt and sugar in all its forms, also fruits or substances that contain any kind of oil. No fruit of any kind. No use of any kind of soap, detergent or chemical and preferably be in a secluded place where there is no contact with people except for the person in charge of taking care of us and feeding us. Traditionally, in the jungle we would just eat boiled or grilled green plantain, rice, oats, toasted corn, some kinds of fish and wild birds. For the most part this is the treatment every curandero ends up prescribing when the sickness cannot be managed only with songs —*icaros*—. The time this type of dieta can last depends on how grave the sickness is and of how much time we need to reestablish our energy, and it also depends on which kind of plants we take during the dieta because there are plants or preparations that require long dietas of three months and others that require short dietas of one week.

One of the most frequent stories told by curanderos is that they did not start on the path of medicine by choice but because a very serious sickness made them decide to diet for long periods of time to recover their health. And in this way they gradually entered the world of plants, receiving the teachings and knowledge that plants brought. When they finished healing themselves, they realized they have walked half of the way to become curanderos.

They say that in ancient times people were not lazy like nowadays and curanderos dieted for many consecutive years achieving great knowledge and powers. Obviously during this time there cannot be any sexual activity, including in dreams. Moreover, dreams are considered a part of reality. Everything that happens during the time of dieta is considered real and important. In a dream, you cannot accept any food or activity that are not allowed. Much of the knowledge one can obtain during a dieta —the use of plants or healing techniques— comes in dreams. There are plants that demand such strict dietas that one must be extremely careful not to 'break' it even in dreams. If we are dieting and we are offered something to eat that is not allowed then we kindly reply we cannot because we are on dieta. All this pressure helps to gain consciousness inside the dream and react adequately. The most important thing is that when one gets used to gain consciousness inside the dream, one has the capacity to know if they are dreaming and can take advantage and ask questions when the spirits of the plants come.

Remembering our vision of the three Andean worlds, the dieta is a prolonged trip to the *Uhu pacha*, that is to say to our interior. During a dieta I clearly felt that abstaining from salt and sugar symbolized retiring from the duality of the mind, of the *Kai pacha*. In an energetic sense it also allowed me to observe —if we consider ourselves as magnetic units— how our life is a permanent exchange of magnetic charges and energies. Major magnetic charges attract minor ones. We are permanently attracted by a numberless of desires —it is not the moment to judge weather they are good or bad—. We are simply attracted by everything our senses perceive. Yielding to the desires discharges us constantly and drains our magnetic charge. On this state we cannot attract anything good. We walk through life being attracted to countless of stimuli —the great science of *marketing*— and this prevents us, with our scarce energy, from keeping the course we have outlined for our life. On the contrary the dieta, by temporary closing the door to the satisfaction of all desire, allows us to recover and increment the magnetic charge without having to go out to search for anything, only letting everything come to our encounter: health, love, prosperity.

Shamans with feathers

Our mental patterns take us to imagine how things could be and when reality does not fit with our speculations we suffer great disappointments. Many people are disenchanted by official religions and their intuition and their good intentions guide them to search for alternatives to connect to the sacred. Unfortunately, due to the little information available they tend to idealize situations and turn them into novels where they are the main character. They travel through the Amazon jungle or through Mexican desserts looking for their 'Don Juan' or a shaman with feathers and big necklaces that will initiate them in their strange rites and pass on wisdom. Nothing is more at odds with reality. At least in Amazonian reality, which is the one I know the most, things are not like that.

The percentage of masters or shamans of a good level that at the same time have an impeccable conduct is really minimal. The truth is that in spite of being heirs to a tradition and having knowledge of healing techniques, many of them are still prisoners of a world of miserable emotions. Jealousy, envy, gossip, slander, energetic attacks and counterattacks are the daily bread. I know very few that have been able to elevate above all this misery. Another very important thing is to have clear discernment between true shamanic science and pure folklore because many times these are mixed and confused. Many people are offering folkloric initiations that do not represent any serious commitment and that distort sacred traditions.

Ten years ago when we opened the ceremonies to people from all around the world, we started doing ayahuasca seminars that included three ceremonies. Only a couple came to the first one, a young man from New Zealand and a Peruvian girl, I have a great friendship with them to this day. When all the participants gathered, the friend from New Zealand asked: 'where is the shaman?' We who knew looked at each other, and trying to avoid laugher and I told him I was going to conduct the ceremony. He took it very badly; he felt he was being scammed. According to the stereotype he had of an ayahuasca ceremony, it was not possible that it would be conducted by someone non indigenous. We tried to give him all the arguments, the 20 years of experience I had, the preparation with a qualified master, in short we offered him everything, we told him to stay at no cost, to participate and then get his conclusions. But no. He had read that this had to be done by an indigenous shaman and if he had feathers so much the better. The couple left —he was somehow outraged— but they came back around two hours later, saying they had thought it over and that they wanted to 'give me an opportunity'. The ceremony happened and it turned out to be a wonderful night so he understood right away that it is not about having feathers but about the relationship one has with this tradition and the respect towards it. Moreover, true Amazonian shamans and curanderos do not wear any feathers. They are the least flashy people one can imagine. They try to pass totally unnoticed. I still remember when we were half way through the ceremony and we could smile a bit —after the first half that was pretty hard—, in the midst of a great silence I asked him: 'so where is the shaman?' It is not a matter of feathers but training and traditional preparation are required so this practice does not get distorted.

Recapitulating

This work is my interpretation of what could be the masterful contribution of the Tawantinsuyo culture to universal culture; a vision of equilibrium and complementarity proved and held for over 5000 years.

To be free and transform ourselves we have to first recognize and then dissolve the mental patterns that condition and limit us. According to our tradition there are three ways to achieve this. The first is with the help of sacred plants, our medicines. The second, with long fasts and dietas, also according to our tradition. And the third, through a deep, sustained and above all, a sincere search for truth inside ourselves; what some people call *the path of the just* or the *Wiraqocha route*.

It is amazing to see how many times we contemplate the truth like the noon sun and moments later we move away and we fall under a layer of clouds when we are not able to hold our clarity. Even the slightest descent of our consciousness is natural, lets try to not justify ourselves or hide behind any sophistry. Lets surround ourselves with symbols that permanently remind us of the purpose of life.

The whole secret is in the memory and in this case memory is consciousness. Without memory we are nothing and we do not even know who we are. Lets not forget to wonder every single day: 'who am I?'

We have a great mother and a great father that according to the tradition of Tawantinsuyo, they are Pachamama and Pachakamaq. It is not so important how we call them. The important thing is they exist. Lets never forget to be grateful to them. Our mother is as sacred as our father and our father is as sacred as our mother. Our mother is being offended with the mistreatment we give her daily. Our way of life has to be consistent with the love a mother deserves.

There are many emotions and they are in the mind. They are the diversity. The feeling is just one and it is love. One heart. Lets remember it is good to think once in a while, but let us never stop feeling. We are beings made to enjoy simultaneity. I think and I feel, therefore I insist. Existence, love and consciousness are the three threads with which we weave our life.

The problem is not in making mistakes; there is nobody that does not make mistakes. The biggest mistake is in not wanting to recognize them. We only have one time to realize. Our greatest enemy is within ourselves and it is called self-deceit. Lets be impeccably honest and get rid of self-deceit. The wheel turns, lets use it, lets transform ourselves.

Follow a sacred path. Do not follow mine, follow your own sacred path. You will see how we run into each other.

Good cannot be imposed like the wicked impose evil. We cannot obligate anybody to follow the path we believe is correct. We can only sing a sacred song and let it resonate in the hearts of those that have enough light to recognize their own path. This is my song.

Ayllumasikunapaq, for all my family.

TAWANTINSUYO 5.0

de Alonso del Río,

Printed in the United States
By Bookmasters